SONIA DELAUNAY
Rhythms and Colours

Jacques Damase

Preface by Michel Hoog

Thames and Hudson · London

The numbers to be found in some of the captions refer
to Sonia Delaunay's personal inventory of her pictures.

The author is greatly indebted to
M. Eduardo Musselier for his courtesy and diligence in
gathering information for texts and captions.

First published in Great Britain in 1972
by Thames and Hudson Ltd, London
© 1971 Hermann, Paris
English translation © 1972 Hermann, Paris

Printed and bound in Switzerland
ISBN 0 500 09087 4

Rhythms and Colours

Contents

Preface

Two contradictory approaches generally tempt historians of modern art. One is to concentrate on those artistic 'movements' as such — Fauvism or Cubism for instance — whose importance, coherence and fruitful results are retrospectively most impressive; the other is to concentrate on individual personalities. Most of those to whom we owe twentieth-century art have had a career too rich in consequences to be defined by a specific episode of their lives, however important it has been. Our epoch has a tendency to revere its great artists and wants to know everything about them; but the danger of emphasizing their individual traits is that one often forgets the historical significance of their work.

In Sonia Delaunay's case the critic has to be even more wary than usual of both temptations. To consider her a great, isolated, unclassifiable figure is to emphasize, quite rightly, her profound originality and her strong personality; but at the same time it is to lose sight of the significance of her personal contribution to twentieth-century art. On the other hand, simply to class her among the Orphic Cubists, as is often done, does not do her justice. She can hardly be said to be a Cubist, and if she is to be called an Orphist one must be very clear about what is meant by the word.

The term Orphism is in current use today in histories of art, for it meets a certain need. Artists classified under this vague label include Sonia Delaunay and Robert Delaunay, as well as Francis Picabia (at least for some of his works) and even Frank Kupka. The term was actually coined by Guillaume Apollinaire to distinguish Robert Delaunay from orthodox Cubists such as Braque and Picasso. The word itself does not therefore permit 11 too precise an interpretation. It is convenient in so far as it shows Sonia Delaunay to have been an active member of the avant-garde prior to the First World War. In the last four centuries, Western art has rarely known periods so revolutionary and so inventive as these years. Cézanne, Gauguin and all the other giants of late nineteenth-century painting had already signed the death warrant of a stifling tradition, and had laid the foundations of a new pictorial art. This was the beginning of a new era of inventiveness in every discipline, and round about 1900 Paris attracted a host of young and energetic people who came from all corners of Europe. Sonia Delaunay was among those who carried the liberating innovations of the older generation through to their logical conclusions, and thereby joined the pioneers of abstract art.

It is not easy today to evaluate the impact of this revolution: abstract painting has won acceptance the world over, from Paris to Tokyo, from Munich to Buenos Aires, from New York to Landerneau. What young artist today does not take himself for a genius for having disfigured a canvas by a couple of wide, slashing strokes? Admittedly we have since had Op art and Pop art, but it is still easy to forget that abstract painting was born more than half a century ago out of the solitary labour of a very few artists who, at least at the start, did not even know of each other's existence. Until about 1940, abstraction remained the preoccupation of a few small groups. It was such a revolutionary new technique that some of the most imaginative artists of the century (a number of well known names could be cited here) approached it without ever really committing themselves, or else abandoned it after a brief experimental phase of no import.

Abstract art was a new way of apprehending reality which was not within the reach of everyone.

For Sonia Delaunay, abstraction has neither been a fortunate accident nor a passing phase; her career has been amazingly coherent (the word 'logical' would be out of place here). Her essential achievement in modern art, although not her only one, has been to liberate colour. This was no minor merit in 1913, at the very moment when Braque and Picasso were preaching the austerity of a monochrome palette, and the Fauves themselves were forgetting their grand flourishes. Sonia Delaunay sought not only to create luminous colour harmonies, but to discover in colour a complete language; with her, colour acquires an independent life of its own. Her entire work, not only that of the years 1910-14, is a poetry of colour; for she believes that painting, as indeed all the plastic arts, must speak to the heart and to the imagination. Colour tones to her are like words to a poet, and she has known how to act upon colours as the poet acts upon words — making them live on the canvas.

This does not mean that Sonia Delaunay has neglected the other elements of her art. Leaving aside the rather academic skill of her first drawings, one needs only to take into consideration the importance of outlines in her work. As a first stage, she had to strip drawing bare of all the remnants of tradition that still clung to it — even in Matisse and the Cubists — so that later she could return to a totally pure form in order to endow it with colour.

Sonia Delaunay has never denied influences. She was familiar with the ideas of Eugène Chevreul, the theorist of colour to whom we owe, among others, the treatise *De la couleur et de l'assor-* 13 *timent des objets colorés considérés d'après cette loi* (On Colour and the Matching of Coloured Objects Considered in Conformity with this Law). It was first published in 1839 and reprinted in 1889. The author had been for many years the Director of the Gobelins tapestry factory, and this study is truly the work of a technician, mainly interested in the matching of varying shades. For instance, there is a chapter on army uniforms, with detailed criticisms of the colour of braids and helmet plumes. In spite of this rather dry side to the treatise, Chevreul also makes a series of subtle observations on the influence of colours upon each other, which lead him to more general conclusions and to his famous law on simultaneous perception of different colours. It was these observations and conclusions that caught the attention of the Neo-Impressionists, of Paul Signac and of Henri Matisse. Possibly the intellectual atmosphere of the turn of the century, swayed by an excessive cult of Science, Rationalism and Progress, unconsciously affected artists who found in Chevreul's theories a systematic scientific justification for their research. But for artists as gifted as Robert and Sonia Delaunay and Blaise Cendrars (later to become the leading light of 'Simultaneism'), it had nothing to do with method. They had adopted the word *simultané* as a banner, and Robert Delaunay had even insisted that the word should remain grammatically invariable. To them the term did not imply the adoption of a theory.

Sonia Delaunay was perfectly aware of the research undertaken by other followers of Chevreul, and has readily acknowledged her debt to them. She has always shown admiration for Georges Seurat's work, and she knew Paul Signac and read his

14   *D'Eugène Delacroix au Néo-Impressionnisme* — a book which was

to have a particularly strong impact on the younger generation. She saw the paintings of Henri-Edmond Cross (a painter whose worth is only now beginning to be recognized), and was quite naturally attracted by his ardent temperament. She was also aware of Gauguin's contribution, as well as that of Van Gogh and Matisse. Nevertheless, it is rather in an international context that one should place her early works. A cross-section of European artistic trends at the beginning of the century is revealing: Art Nouveau (also called Jugendstil, Liberty, Modern Style and Style Nouille) was a typical international occurrence; similarly the vast wave of colourful Expressionism which unfurled immediately after. Between 1905 and 1910 many French, German and Russian artists passed through a Fauve or Expressionist period, even though later they were to follow very divergent paths. It manifested itself first in France, with Edvard Munch and the French Fauves. Soon German groups followed suit, without, however, giving up any of their own originality. After leaving her native Russia, Sonia first passed through Karlsruhe before coming to Paris, and her work between 1905 and 1908 is clearly marked by this phase. The colours employed (blues, oranges and purplish shades), and the synthetic style of drawing, are truly hers; but, without diminishing her originality in any way, one can note that her researches were by no means isolated. Robert Delaunay wrote many years later, that his wife came under the influence of two strong currents: a Parisian one, which had Gauguin and Matisse as its mentors, and a 'Slavonic colour' one which appears in the works of artists as different as Kandinsky and Jawlensky, and later in Malevich and Chagall.

With Sonia Delaunay, this language of colour was quick to

mature. It became a complete language which, paradoxically, allowed her to express reality with greater insight the further she moved away from representation. This evolution was all the more remarkable in that, chronologically speaking, it took place at the very moment when Cubism (whose starting-point was not so different from hers) was achieving quite opposite results. Youth and movement, life in all its vitality, have never lost their hold upon Sonia Delaunay. Her *Flamenco Dancers*, her collaboration with Serge Diaghilev, her theatre and film costumes, are all evidence of her love of dance and of the theatre. In 1913, the dance inspired one of her major works, the *Bal Bullier* (Musée National d'Art Moderne, Paris), a large canvas more than ten feet wide. At the top of the Boulevard Saint-Michel and facing the Closerie des Lilas, the Bal Bullier was the pre-war rendezvous of artists and writers. There one could dance the fashionable tango, considered lewd and shocking by many. The subject itself was right up to date: but more original and more revolutionary still was the manner with which Sonia Delaunay treated it, producing a modern version of a traditional theme used by Rubens in his *Kermesse* and by Renoir in his *Moulin de la Galette*. Even in Degas and Toulouse-Lautrec, the dancers moved under artificial lighting and were caught in specific poses, arbitrarily chosen for their expressiveness by an artist who is a spectator. Here, for the first time, we have a synthesis of coloured movements, of dancing couples, portrayed by an artist who is a participator, and who refuses to analyse movement. The result is an over-all impression, with all the imprecision and lack of finish that this implies, just as if one had asked a dancer to

describe the decor of the dance-hall from memory. It was only many years later that a similar degree of subjectivity was attained in fields as diverse as the novel and the cinema (take for instance the dance-hall scene in *West Side Story*).

The other major canvas of this period, the *Electric Prisms* of 1914 (Musée National d'Art Moderne, Paris), can be viewed in the same context. The new electric street lighting and the first illuminated advertisements had caught Sonia Delaunay's imagination. Since the 1900 Universal Exhibition, whose most striking feature had been electric lighting effects, Paris had acquired the reputation of being the 'City of Light'. Sonia Delaunay was fascinated by the coloured shimmer of the street lights on rainy days. Once more, the modernity of her approach was very different from that of the Fauves, whose audacities, more often than not, were restricted to conventional themes. Sonia Delaunay, then living in the Rue des Grands-Augustins, made countless studies of these lighting phenomena along the Boulevard Saint-Michel and in front of the fountain in the Place Saint-Michel. One might be tempted to consider these studies as mere colour notations; in fact, they bear witness to a new way of apprehending reality which was unique at the time. Moreover, the artist always attached a great deal of importance to these rough sketches. Long before it had become fashionable to exhibit preliminary drawings, she exhibited them at Stockholm in 1917 and at Bilbao in 1919. Back in her studio, she pursued her work with gouaches, pastels and paper cut-outs, before attempting the large eight-foot-square canvas which she exhibited at the 1914 Salon des Indépendants; it is a eulogy of light, or, as the artist would have put it, of colour-light. The transposition of movement into colour, the decomposition of 17 light, prismatic haloes dancing around electric bulbs, all become the vehicle of a dazzling poetry — a new pictorial language to translate one of the most spectacular inventions of the modern world. In this Sonia Delaunay was far ahead (and not only chronologically) of Fernand Léger and Raoul Dufy, who knew how to use the themes of our mechanized society in their paintings, but who never looked, as she did, for a formal equivalent. It was only with the advent of kinetic art, whose inventors have always recognized their indebtedness to Sonia Delaunay, that an artistic equivalent of the lights of Saint-Lazare or of Broadway was found.

The only artist of that epoch whose approach was in any way analogous to hers was of course Robert Delaunay, particularly in his *Pigs' Merry-go-round* and his *Homage to Blériot*. Both of them chose their themes from modern life; both transposed these into a new plastic language. Their works represent a clean break with that tradition, apparent even in Cubism, which presupposes the position of the artist to be fixed in relation to his subject. For the artist's 'observation', Robert and Sonia Delaunay substituted the instantaneous and blurred over-all 'perception' of the passer-by. Again and again they manifested their common vision; and this largely answers the question of who influenced whom. Every artist, even the greatest, comes under a number of influences. These can be momentary, can be related to a specific aspect of his art, or again can be in the form of an impulse, an invitation to follow a new path. A great artist loses none of his originality by this; on the contrary, such an influence may even lead him to deeper self-realization.

18   As for the Delaunays, when one does discern the influence

of the one upon the other, it implies more than a superficial similarity: it implies the choice of an analogous approach. Robert Delaunay's *Pigs' Merry-go-round* and *Homage to Blériot*, like Sonia's *Electric Prisms*, were preceded by a large number of sketches and studies. This demonstrates that in each case the technique employed was conscious and voluntary, corresponding to a fundamental artistic vision, and not the result of a fortuitous, momentary experimental similarity.

The discovery of abstraction by both husband and wife can be considered in the same light. Today, the birth of abstract painting is still subject to controversy; it has not yet entered the domain of undisputed historical fact. Periodically one hears of some unknown artist who before 1905 had executed works bearing no reference to the external world. In so far as we can firmly establish the date of these works and prove that they are not experimental flukes, their principal interest is to demonstrate that the idea was 'in the air'. Indeed, there are many other historically more convincing cases of artists who even before 1900 came very close to abstraction. One can quote here artists such as Odilon Redon, Henri van de Velde, Gustave Moreau and Paul Cézanne.

The remarkable fact in the cases of both Sonia and Robert Delaunay is the coherence of their progress towards abstraction. The stages passed through by Robert Delaunay are easily distinguishable: first, his so-called destructive period, still closely related to Cubism, with the dislocation of forms in a play of lights; then the decomposition of colours, the analysis of refracted light and the elaboration of a new pictorial language in the course of 1912 with series such as *City of Paris, Windows* and 19 the first of his *Circular Forms*. Thus in the space of seven years, from 1905 to 1912, Delaunay passed through Neo-Impressionism, skirted Fauvism (though he was younger than any of the Fauves), and became one of the major figures of the pre-Cubism of the years 1905 to 1910 whose leaders were all, with the exception of Picasso, lapsed Fauves like Braque, Derain and Dufy. In his views of *Saint-Séverin* of 1909-10, Robert Delaunay departed from strict Cubism and showed a growing interest in problems of light and colour. At about this time he met and married Sonia Terk. A much-quoted text by Robert Delaunay, written twenty years later, still bears the impact of his enthusiasm when he discovered in Sonia the 'anarchical fiery spirit (in relation to colour) which was later to be transformed into controlled energy'.

Rather than saying that Sonia influenced Robert, it would be more accurate to say that she showed him the way to pure colour which best suited the requirements of abstraction. Robert Delaunay's development towards abstract art was far too coherent and too clear-cut for us to imagine that Sonia influenced him totally; and the fact that he was inspired by her does nothing to diminish the powerfulness or the dazzling beauty and lyricism of his *Suns* and *Circular Forms* of 1912-14. It is, moreover, most likely that impulses went both ways. Would it not be simpler to note in both a common attitude, a common artistic development? Guillaume Apollinaire, who was their guest for a time, used to say that 'they talk painting from the moment they awake'. It is not surprising that this couple, so united in every way, should have found perfect understanding in what mattered most to them, their painting.

Robert and Sonia Delaunay had the joint ambition to free

their art from those exclusive cliques within which the most advanced activities in modern art were often imprisoned. In Portugal in 1917, and in 1937 at the time of the Universal Exhibition, Sonia Delaunay executed vast murals. She also had the opportunity to work for the theatre and, in 1926, for the cinema. But it is more particularly in the design of utilitarian objects that, very early on, her creative spirit found its best expression. In 1911, soon after the birth of her son Charles, the future jazz historian, she made a patchwork blanket out of pieces of material. The experiment was so successful, as she herself admits, that it incited her to go further in this line. In the years to come, she made a series of other objects: caskets, lamp-shades, book-covers, clothes. All of these mark the introduction of her art, and with it of the avant-garde, into everyday life.

This period, about 1913, also saw her illustrations for Blaise Cendrars's *Prose du Transsibérien et de la petite Jehanne de France*, the originality of which is worth mentioning briefly. Thanks to the encouragement of Ambroise Vollard and D.H. Kahnweiler, artists like Bonnard, Derain and Dufy had already begun to revolutionize this domain with illustrations of texts such as Apollinaire's *Bestiaire ou cortège d'Orphée* (the title of which may have been the origin of the word 'Orphism') and *L'Enchanteur pourrissant*. However, owing probably to the influence of Apollinaire — a book-lover, an habitué of the Bibliothèque Mazarine and of the Bibliothèque Nationale — the layout of these books resembles more a return to the grand tradition than a step forward. The *Prose du Transsibérien*, on the contrary, combines in a strikingly original layout — the book is a gigantic six-foot folded strip — a revolutionary style of illustration, a text which breaks with conventional prosody, and a dislocated typography which makes use of more than a dozen different founts of type.

We owe this extraordinary achievement, in which image and text are united, to the mutual admiration and friendship of Blaise Cendrars and Sonia Delaunay. The book was immediately to find an enthusiastic advocate in Apollinaire. Seldom associating with other artists, the Delaunays were often surrounded by poets: Apollinaire, Cendrars, Tristan Tzara, Philippe Soupault, Aragon, André Breton, Paul Eluard, Vladimir Mayakovsky, Jean Delteil, Iliazd, Jean Cocteau, and many others. In some cases the relationship was only transitory, but in others, as with Tzara and Delteil, a deep and lasting friendship was established.

It was again in collaboration with Blaise Cendrars that in 1914 Sonia Delaunay designed a series of advertising posters, for which Cendrars provided the copy. Unfortunately, none of these projects were ever used, though they have lost none of their impact even today. In many modern street and press advertisements one can recognize the influence of the language of colour invented by Sonia Delaunay.

In the years that followed she instigated many other projects: book-covers (for André Salmon's *Propos d'atelier*, for instance), covers of periodicals (such as *Ararat* and *Abstraction-Création*) and literally thousands of designs for materials and clothes — on which Sonia Delaunay largely concentrated between 1917 and 1930. These designs have dated so little that lately a number of them have been re-used. In the last few years she has published several important albums of engravings, mostly illustrating poetic texts, as well as a pack of playing-cards for which the artist has entirely re-designed the images. Sonia Delaunay's unflagging interest in all forms of the applied arts reveals a deep commitment. And still I have not mentioned everything: there are also stained-glass windows, carpets, tapestries and mosaics.

These different ventures were carried out with total seriousness and meticulous care. In each case the artist applied herself to learn, or to rediscover, the laws governing each technique. Moreover, all these activities have this in common: they are a challenge to the monopoly of easel painting in artistic production. Of course, Sonia Delaunay has never ceased painting canvases and gouaches; but it is remarkable that so large a part of her activities have lain outside this sphere. Nineteenth-century artists (even the most independent, like Manet and Cézanne) never completely succeeded in liberating themselves from the traditional concept of easel painting. One of the most characteristic traits of contemporary artistic production is precisely the extreme diversity of artistic media, and Sonia Delaunay must certainly be counted among those who have done much to bring about this change. Moreover, all her ventures result from her desire to bring art to a wider public. Thus, with Sonia Delaunay, modern art becomes part of the pageantry of the street, and enters even into the most familiar objects in the home. For Sonia Delaunay this preoccupation with the applied arts existed from a very early stage of her career; it is the very essence of her art.

Admired by the artists of the following generation, who have acknowledged the importance of her contribution to modern art, and who have often felt her influence, Sonia Delaunay has never ceased to pursue her researches. Her recent works display a use of completely new colours which show just how much she refuses to be hemmed in by formulas, or to repeat her previous 23 successes; but they also display the same lyricism, the same warmth and the same freedom that mark her earlier works.

Thus, from whatever angle one approaches it, Sonia Delaunay's art has always belonged to its own time, and thus to ours. What is more, like the poets whom she has admired, Sonia Delaunay has often heralded some of those aspirations which are felt most deeply today. In a world where it has become commonplace to say that more progress has been made in the last sixty years than in the last five centuries, we are fortunate that poets and artists have lived who have been able to trace its new profile. Sonia Delaunay is to be counted among them.

Michel Hoog

Beginnings

St. Petersburg. Sonia Delaunay's childhood world. On the left, the Winter Palace and the Alexander column; above, the Senate.

St. Petersburg. The Fontaka quay; façades of
eighteenth- and nineteenth-century mansions.

Sonia Terk as a child. On the left in 1893, aged eight;
on the right, at a fancy-dress ball when she was twelve.

The Laundress.
St. Petersburg, 1904.
Charcoal heightened with
white, on paper.
48 × 29 cm; no. 531.

Finnish Peasant.
Finland, 1904.
Charcoal and chalk on paper.
29 × 22 cm; no. 526.
Musée National d'Art
Moderne, Paris.

The Artist's Aunt.
1904. Charcoal and chalk on paper.
48 × 30 cm; no. 523.

Head of a Little Girl.
Finland, 1904.
Charcoal and chalk on grey paper.
40 × 30 cm; no. 522.
Musée National d'Art
Moderne, Paris.

Self-portrait.
Finland, 1904.
Charcoal on paper.
48.5 × 31 cm; no. 1441.

32

onia Terk in St. Petersburg in 1901.

Sonia Terk at Fontainebleau and in Finland in 1905.

Summer holiday, 1903-1904;
postcard of the Black River
on the Russo-Finnish border.

Finnish landscape
Finland, 1906.
Watercolour. 28.5 × 78.5 cm; no. 78.

Finnish landscape. Finland, 1906. Oil on canvas. 20.5 × 28.5 cm; no. 73.

Early works

The memories of the little girl who lived in the Ukrainian plains are memories of colour and light. Along a path between walls of snow the little girl goes out to fetch her father home for lunch. All around, long, low, white houses. Soon winter passes, and the endless, rolling countryside is ablaze with sunlight; nature is resplendent, manifesting her faith in life, and in her thick, rich soil; melons and watermelons grow; fields of red tomatoes encircle the farms; gigantic sunflowers, deep gold with black centres, reach up to a clear sky. Carts roll by, drawn by the same swift, strong horses which had pulled the tinkling sleighs through the snow. Everything is vast, boundless, and full of a joy which makes us think of Gogol, another child of this land. Later, a large deserted beach on the shores of the Baltic sea; and the same little girl, five years old, picking up pieces of amber in the fine white sand.

Later still, St. Petersburg, with its wide avenues. The city founded by Peter the Great, where it was considered a mark of good breeding to converse in French or German, and where Pushkin, sensing the talent of Gogol, had taken him in hand and inspired him to write. It might seem strange to link Sonia Terk with Gogol, yet in both we encounter the same profound passion for their country, the same sense of colour, and the same love of life tinged with melancholy.

Winter walks through the city frequently led Sonia to those fairgrounds which, from Bakst's stage sets for *Petrouchka,* we can picture so well. There, old men used to narrate the immemorial Russian legends; they had long white beards, and the green and blue lights which lit them up made them strange and wonderful. The little girl was already thirsting for new sights. Another favourite spot was the Summer Garden, peopled with its poetic world of marble statues.

Her bedroom, which was big enough to be a studio, was dominated by a great white porcelain stove that gave out a peculiar glow in the evening. There was also blue furniture, an oval-shaped painting of the Italian school, and a deep divan. In the ballroom there were three large fireplaces, and numerous paintings. Other paintings of the Realist school hung in the drawing-room: a view of Amsterdam in the rain; a scene set in Morocco, depicting a woman draped in flimsy veils outlining the curves of her body; a vast landscape in the middle of which stood a gipsy woman carrying a child. All this was certainly somewhat trite, but nonetheless unpretentious; it was a time when people bought pictures not for the prestige of a signature but because they liked them.

Sonia was brought up in a musical atmosphere; her aunt sang German *Lieder,* and her cousin played popular operatic arias on the piano. Until she was fourteen, she was taught by three governesses concurrently, one German, one English and one French; she was thus able at an early age, to read Goethe, Shakespeare and Voltaire in the original, as well as all of Dostoyevsky. At St. Petersburg at this time, the works of Baudelaire and Verlaine were already well known.

Thanks to Catherine the Great, the Winter Palace and the Hermitage house some of the best picture collections in the world, a sanctuary for those large Rembrandts which Sonia remembers seeing there. She can also recall the many paintings in her uncle's library and in the reception rooms, as well as 38 innumerable albums of engravings reproducing Italian and

Flemish masterpieces, leafed through while adults were immersed in after-dinner talk. After-dinner talk . . . from breakfast at eight until dinner at six one did not seem to stop eating. Sonia recalls special celebratory dinners, with a thirteen-foot-long table laden with hors-d'œuvres of all sorts, caviare, sausage, hams, cheeses. After this the meal really began: borsch with pirozhki, then smoked fish with vegetable salad, followed by poultry or game, finally desserts, and, with all this, French or Hungarian wines. Two or three hours later tea was served, accompanied by enormous round cakes rich with nuts and chocolate. Their cook was famous, the best in the city after the Tsar's.

The child longed to paint; that was the most important thing to her. The high-school art teacher (a lady who was later to found the Museum of Popular Art) advised her family to let her talent develop by sending her abroad. It was essential that she should be able to live a life where she could realize her full potential; in the ancient city of the Tsars this was not possible. Aged eighteen, with a brilliant high-school career behind her, she was allowed to leave for Germany. The year was now 1903. Revolution was near, but Sonia has no recollection of social unrest. She admits that she has never had any love for politics, or for revolutions (except personal ones). She left St. Petersburg behind, almost relieved, hardly sorry even to part from the masterpieces which she loved, from the treasures of Kazan Cathedral and its icons. The memories of these were nevertheless to remain with her throughout her life.

In 1903 Professor Schmidt-Reuter was teaching in Karlsruhe. He was an excellent teacher and gave her a solid grounding, enabling her to avoid a false, academic approach to art. For two winters she studied under his guidance. She sometimes saw Arnold Schönberg, who was also at the Academy. Freed from the oppressive bourgeois opulence of St. Petersburg, she could now begin to breathe and discover her own vitality. After reading Julius Meier-Graefe's book on the Impressionists, she had only one desire: to go and live in the country which gave birth to the *Oarsmen* and the *Moulin de la Galette*. She felt in those works a certain lightness quite foreign to the German spirit.

In 1905, when she had just turned twenty, she arrived in Paris and settled down in a Left Bank *pension* with four other Russian girls. In no time, twenty or so friends were meeting every evening in her room. She enrolled at La Palette, a school where her teachers, all well established neo-classicists, were Cottet, Aman-Jean, Desvallières, Simon and Jacques-Emile Blanche. Each corrected the pupil's work in turn, with the result that no one quite knew what to do. From then on Sonia always worked alone.

During a holiday in Finland after leaving Karlsruhe, she did a charcoal drawing of an old peasant and a little girl. She also drew a portrait of the aunt who had brought her up, but for whom she could feel no true affection — for fear, perhaps, of intrusion into her inner self. Her first Paris painting, *Philomène*, is dated 1907. In spite of her admiration for the Impressionists, she felt drawn to pure colour. The colours of her childhood, of the Ukraine and its colourful peasant weddings, with the red and green beribboned dance-dresses. She also recalled memories of an album of traditional costumes which her uncle had once brought back from Sweden. In *Philomène* one can see how she had already thrown off the constraints of her bourgeois education.

The artistic vision is liberated, and so are the colours; Van Gogh's and Gauguin's influence is still present.

At this time she was working in a studio in the Rue Campagne-Première. Gauguin, who was already beginning to be known in artistic circles in Paris, was holding an exhibition in the Rue Laffitte. Near the Madeleine, Sonia admired Vuillard and Bonnard in the windows of the Galerie Bernheim-Jeune. She also discovered Matisse; but, except for the large still-lifes, she and the other Russian girls found his vision still too conventional and bourgeois. In the Rue Laffitte too, at Vollard's and at Sagot's, she saw numerous paintings — and even drawings by Rodin — sold for the equivalent of ten of today's francs.

The Ile Saint-Louis: the Quai aux Fleurs. This was the subject of one of her first engravings. In the flat below her lived the German critic Wilhelm Uhde. Their common love of art brought them together, and in his home she admired magnificent Fauve paintings as well as canvases by Braque, Derain, Vlaminck and Dufy; she was dazzled. Much impressed by this cultured man who knew so much about art, she finally married him in London in 1909. At that time she was busy painting a still-life much in the style of Derain. She also worked on a piece of embroidery, *Foliage,* in shades of green and grey (hardly her colours!). The influence of the Douanier Rousseau was nevertheless already present. In the privacy of his gallery in the Rue Notre-Dame des Champs, Wilhelm Uhde displayed his Braques, his Picassos and his Rousseaus to a few connoisseurs. Sometimes a young artist by the name of Robert Delaunay wandered in.

During the winter of 1909, in the nearly empty galleries of the Louvre which house Egyptian and Chaldean art, a young 41 couple passed spellbound from one masterpiece to another. These two solitary visitors were Sonia Uhde and Robert Delaunay; they were to be married before long.

This marriage was an important event at a crucial period in the history of modern art. This meeting of two great artists — the western rationalism of the one and the East European warmth of the other, combined in one shared life's work — was more than a meeting and a collaboration. Robert and Sonia Delaunay expressed their love for each other through their art, as other famous couples have expressed their love for each other through faith or through poetry. When they met, Robert Delaunay had recently abandoned Neo-Impressionism. He had discovered Chevreul's theories in 1904-05, after a Breton period. Under Cézanne's influence, he had painted the *Saint-Séverin* series and had started on a set of still-lifes, landscapes and self-portraits. People were later to consider his *Towers* and his *Cities* as revelations — and him as an innovator. After painting his *Large City of Paris* (1912), which brought to a close his Cubist period, he painted his first *Windows* and created his first 'simultaneous discs'. These were to lead him to the type of painting, freed from all efforts at representation, that he called 'pure painting'. Sonia discovered with him the prismatic forms of his first attempts. According to the critic Gualteri di San Lazzaro, she brought to their common work her personal stamp, recognizable even in the first discs.

'For me', said Sonia, 'Delaunay was a poet, but one who wrote in colours and not in words. We lived like children. We both still had private incomes in those days, and we played at living,
42 as children play with dolls.

'My childhood had been exceptionally stable; that was the reason why I had left Russia.

'Before 1900. social and economic life was conventional. Things only began to change round about 1905, when the French middle class was already far ahead in terms of progress.

'Even though I played cowboys and Indians under the tables with my imaginative German governess, more like a boy than a girl, and even though my uncle was more affectionate than my aunt, there still existed a tremendous barrier in those days between parents and children . . .

'My life then was very beautiful, for it was made up of dreams. It suddenly seemed very sordid when I found out that I had to earn a living. Delaunay was for ever elaborating the wildest business plans, and spoke of them quite marvellously. I loved this side of him; it was so very different from what I had known earlier in the traditional context of the upper middle class. With him, business became a poetic thing.'

The Delaunays first lived near Nantua with their forty birds (which they later brought with them to Paris). Their son was born there in 1911. Sonia made him a patchwork blanket like those of Russian peasant women. When completed, the layout of the pieces of cloth so resembled a Cubist composition that she then tried to apply the idea to other objects.

They moved back to Paris. To their studio in the Rue des Grands-Augustins came a constant flow of visitors: the fashionable world, artists, all nationalities. Among them was the poet Tchouïko, of whom Sonia did two portraits and one engraving. 'He was really ugly, but his eyes were full of dreams. He visited me both before and after my marriage. In fact all my friends 43 became friends of Delaunay, and one of them, Mrs. Epstein, introduced Delaunay to Kandinsky, who invited him to the Blaue Reiter exhibition in Munich.'

At about the time of the theft of the *Mona Lisa*, another well known poet came to seek refuge with them. Guillaume Apollinaire had been suspected of this theft, and of that of some statuettes which had been found at his secretary's home. While all his friends were deserting him, the Delaunays put him up in their studio, which was on the same landing as their flat, until the charges against him were dismissed. Delaunay was then busy painting his first *Window*, a work which inspired Apollinaire to write his famous poem 'Les Fenêtres'. It was also during this period that he began his novel *Les Mormons*. Sonia recalls:

'It was a real pleasure to have Apollinaire eat with us; he was a great eater and appreciated good cooking. After dinner we often went for walks in the neighbourhood, which was very peaceful in those days. Strolling in the middle of the street, Apollinaire would recite his latest poems; on other evenings he would read us passages of a novel he was writing about the Mormons. In December 1912 he moved into 202 Boulevard Saint-Germain, and I made him short muslin curtains in 'simultaneous' colours. He mentions these in one of his literary chronicles, published in the *Mercure de France*.

'Entrenched between red and green, the yellow fades away
When sing the parakeets in their native forests.'

Like Apollinaire, the Delaunays were fascinated by the Douanier Rousseau. Delaunay often went to visit him. Many years later, Sonia opened a file and, one by one, held up the documents which it contained saying, 'See, these are photographs which the Douanier had taken of his paintings.' The photographs were yellowed with age, gummed on a sheet of cardboard surrounded by a floral design and annotated in Delaunay's handwriting. Each document awakened a memory. Contemplating the famous *Cart with the White Horse,* she recalled:

'In the summer of 1911, we were taking a walk in Meudon — in those days one did not go very far away on holiday — and we discovered, in a grocery shop, two magnificent paintings by Rousseau: this cart, and a white rabbit with carrots. Apollinaire, who at that particular time was richer than us, bought them. Rousseau had exchanged these paintings for food!

'Here is his famous *Snake Charmer.* Delaunay's mother had commissioned it from Rousseau. She had described her trip to India and he, inspired by her stories, had painted this vast canvas, which is one of his masterpieces.

'Who was Rousseau? For us he was the typical French petit bourgeois, always correctly dressed, always standing on his dignity. He was extremely proud of being Monsieur Henri Rousseau, retired customs official. Yet painting was more than a hobby to him: it was his passion.

'From his hospital bed, when already dying of gangrene in the leg, he was still asking Delaunay questions. The series of canvases which Delaunay had painted of the Eiffel Tower, viewed simultaneously from different angles, intrigued him. "But how did you manage to see it like this?" he inquired.

'He was never really influenced by his artist friends; modern art was something curious and incomprehensible to him.

'After Rousseau's death in 1910 the contents of his studio were dispersed and sold. Delaunay bought several canvases which we then sold in order to give him at least a decent burial; his body had been placed in a pauper's grave. A little before the Second World War, when we went back to the cemetery to renew the upkeep charges we looked for Alfred Jarry's grave too, in memory of Rousseau who had painted him. No one had looked after it and his remains had been dispersed. Today, Rousseau lies in the centre of a square at Laval, where he was born. He would certainly have liked the spot.'

Sonia Delaunay likes to talk about the Douanier Rousseau. When asked what he really represented for her and her husband, she replied that what attracted her was that he was so true to himself; he was the epitome of the suburban Frenchman. It was through his eyes that they saw the French suburbs of that epoch. For them, Rousseau remained the honest and simple man that he was. Apollinaire composed an epitaph, which Brancusi then engraved on his tombstone.

In January 1913 Delaunay and Apollinaire went to Berlin together — Apollinaire to give a lecture on modern art, and Delaunay to mount an exhibition at the Sturm gallery. On their way back they stopped for twenty-four hours in Bonn to see August Macke, with whom they found much in common.

In about 1913 the municipality of Paris had the old street lights changed for more modern ones, beginning with those on the Boulevard Saint-Michel. Another sign of the times was that the election posters began to vie with each other in the violent colours which they displayed.

This was the beginning of a new era — an era of light and

colour. In the course of their walks through the city, Sonia and Robert Delaunay loved looking at the multi-coloured haloes round the street lights. They gave Delaunay the idea of observing the moon, where he found the same kind of haloes; and when he looked at the sun he found it covered with spots in the shape of discs. From then on, he gave up the prismatic colour of his famous *Windows*, in favour of circular forms, which were to lead him to his pure discs.

Sonia, for her part, inspired by the coloured election posters, set down her impressions in bright pencil strokes. These studies resemble in many ways the work of Hans Hartung, though they are gayer. In spite of her researches, Sonia does away with theories when she paints, seeking complete spontaneity. Her work before the First World War was crowned by her *Electric Prisms* (1914), a canvas which has the same dimensions as Robert Delaunay's *Pigs' Merry-go-round*. It was her observation of electric lighting that led to the execution of this painting. Here, movement expressed through colour and the analysis of decomposed light are the sources of a dazzling poetry — the same vivid poetry of modernity which radiates from the *Bal Bullier*. Blaise Cendrars explains this phenomenon in perhaps the clearest terms: 'Colour is a sensuous element. The senses are reality. That is why the world is coloured. The senses build. Then intelligence arises. Colours sing. By neglecting colour the Cubists neglected the emotional grounds of a work of art —that sensuous, irrational, absurd, lyrical element which brings a painting to life surrealistically.'

Every Thursday the Delaunays and their friends, painters and poets, met at the Bal Bullier to dance the fox-trot and the tango among students and *midinettes*. The smooth undulations of the tango are re-enacted through the medium of colour in the *Bal Bullier* and the *Electric Prisms*. There are several small-scale versions of the *Bal Bullier*, as well as the large canvas which hangs in the Musée d'Art Moderne in Paris. With the *Prisms*, this painting is a work of capital importance for its period. Sonia Delaunay has more affinities with Degas than with any other of her immediate predecessors who made use of the theme of dancing. But even in Degas the representation of dance movement remains part of an intellectual process; there is a break in the continuity between the figure and the background against which the poised ballerina stands out. Sonia Delaunay is more faithful to the raw data of perception; she mingles planes, superimposes attitudes, in order to reproduce the very sensations of the dizzy dancers. The researches of the Futurists, who expressed movement by decomposing it, were also quite foreign to her own vision.

Every Wednesday Apollinaire used to receive his friends in his new flat on the Boulevard Saint-Germain. On one occasion they met a shy young man called Blaise Cendrars who, the following day, came to show them his poem *Pâques*. They were struck by his talent, and immediately Sonia Delaunay set about making a binding for the poem.

'From then onward he came to lunch nearly every day,' she recalls. 'He used to live close by at 4 Rue de Savoie in those days. He soon became part of our circle. His poetry was his life, and he lived for it, as Delaunay and myself lived for our painting. A few weeks later he wrote the *Transsibérien*, and, overwhelmed by the beauty of this poem, I undertook to illustrate it. The book was six a half feet long and was printed by *pochoir*. Cendrars and

I chose the different faces and sizes of type in which it was to be printed — a real innovation in those days.

'This was the dawn of a new vision of the world which, in fine art as in poetry, was to revolutionize traditional ideas. Creative intensity was so much part of our lives that none of us were even capable of hypocrisy — the key to rapid success among many of our contemporaries. Affectation, publicity, these never even occurred to me when I was busy making my "simultaneous" dresses out of fragments of coloured material; the resulting variegated colours made quite a sensation at the time.'

Many years later Sonia Delaunay wrote in the *Mercure de France*:

'Cendrars' death distressed me deeply. It shadowed one of the most luminous moments of my life. Slowly but surely people will come to pay homage to him as one of the truest and greatest poets of our time.'

Blaise Cendrars makes the following instructive comment about his book and the state of mind in which he wrote it:

'I am not a poet. I am a libertine. I don't have a specific method when I work. I have a sex. I am far too sensitive. I don't know how to speak about myself objectively. Every living being has a physiology, and writing is probably as necessary to me as eating, breathing and singing. It may be an instinctive need; it may be a spiritual one. *Pange lingua.* Animals have so many idiosyncrasies! Perhaps it is also a discipline to incite me to live better — all this and more.

'Literature is not set apart from life. It is life. Writing is no profession, just as living is no profession. Therefore, there are no artists. Living organisms do not work . . . Specialization doesn't exist. I am no man of letters. I dislike sloggers and social climbers. What is a school of thought? In Greece, or in Sing Sing gaol, I would most probably write quite differently. As it happens, I have written my best poems in cities where five million people live or, haunted by games played in childhood, five thousand leagues under the sea with Jules Verne to keep me company. A life is a poem in motion . . . The *Prose du Trans-sibérien* is therefore truly a poem, being part of the life of a libertine. It is his love, his passion, his vice, his greatness, his outpouring! It is part of himself, his dream, the 'rib he has torn from his side. It is mortal, wounded by too much love, pregnant. Terrifying laughter. Life, more life: with reds, blues, dreams, blood — like the tales narrated from times immemorial.

'I like legends, discussions, language mistakes, detective stories, the bodies of girls, the sun, the Eiffel Tower, ruffians — and the crafty Continental who, facetiously, delights in modernity — all of it! What am I heading for? How should I know, I, who never even set foot in a museum! I was born a prodigal . . .

'This is what I was intent on saying: I have a fever. That is why the art of the Delaunays so attracts me; it is so full of sun, of instants of violence lashing out, roaring. Madame Delaunay has made such a magnificent book of colours that my poem is drenched in light, even more than my own life. This fills me with joy. Its extraordinary dimensions too: imagine, six and a half feet long!'

It was Delaunay's idea that a text should accompany the poem. When the book appeared in October 1913 the periodicals and newspaper columns were full of it, due largely to a publicity

handout written by Blaise Cendrars and illustrated by Sonia

Delaunay. In the *Soirées de Paris* of 15 June 1914, Guillaume Apollinaire wrote: 'The combined work of Blaise Cendrars and Sonia Delaunay-Terk is one of the first attempts to achieve simultaneity with contrasts written in colours. Their aim is to teach the eye to read the poem at a single glance, as the conductor reads a page of an orchestral score, as one assimilates in one instant the pattern of a poster.'

This is what Blaise Cendrars wrote about Sonia Delaunay's painting and about the new meaning given to the word 'simultaneous':

'We look up to the sun. This is not a black and white contrast, a dissimilarity; on the contrary. Today's art seeks depth. The word "simultaneous" is a technical term. . . .

'Simultaneity is a technique, and simultaneous contrast is the most recent improvement brought to this technique. This simultaneous contrast is experienced depth — reality — form — construction — representation — life. Depth is the new inspiration.'

Robert Delaunay, who was in fact one of her first biographers and critics, explained the revolution that Sonia brought about in the field of colour through her racial origins: 'Like all artists and poets from the East, she has a hereditary bent for colour. One already feels this lyricism, this need to express herself through colours — dazzling, yet still timid and uncertain — in her first studies done on her own or under the supervision of a teacher.

'Her understanding of colour went beyond the academic and official teaching which she had received. It was motivated by an instinctive need incompatible with formulas, and by a mettle later to be harnessed and transformed into controlled strength.

In her early works, her subjects were chosen at random, as in the paintings which date from 1907, portrait of an Italian woman, young girl lying down, portrait of Mme Minsky, and so on. It is already clear that these are the works of a born colourist; colour is still enslaved by the line, by traditional chiaroscuro, but nevertheless it dazzles with the glaze of enamel, ceramics or the sheen of carpets. By this is meant that already there is a feeling for surface combining, so to speak, successively on the canvas. There is a store of pictorial energy as yet unexploited; ancient modes of expression — I mean a somewhat primitive conception of traditional methods — and the rather barbaric, almost caricatural, expression of her portraits, which clashed with the academic platitudes of the day and added a dash of piquancy to French art. It was the hey-day of Fauvism, and Gauguinism, or exoticism, flourished at the Indépendants. Matisse upheld the banner of French taste at this time, by channelling this avalanche of Slavonic and Oriental painting and seasoning it with the Parisian literary taste of the moment. This was a neo-Baudelairian epoch, the age of *Woman in Green Hat*, of *Luxe, calme et volupté*, and so forth.'

The year 1909 brought a change. Sonia Delaunay designed some tapestries which showed that she was about to abandon perspective. From 1912 or thereabouts, her work began to show evidences of a new kind of colour, which was free from conventions. We see this in her bookbindings of contemporary poetry and in her colourful lampshades. These were her first experimental steps in a direction bound for the unknown.

Apart from the *Transsibérien* and the binding for *Pâques*, carried out for Cendrars — favourite topics with the journalists who wrote about the 1913 Cubist Exhibition — Sonia also exhibited a 'simultaneous' book in which both cover and content were composed of combined fragments of paper. These bindings are the first purely non-figurative *papiers collés*. In creating them she was more interested by the desire to discover free plastic analogies with the emotions which the texts aroused, than by mere decoration. She was already intrigued by the quality of texture when she made the blanket for her son's cot; she was not governed by texture, but used it to combine colour values. Her compositions done with cut-out segments of circles, triangles and lozenges reveal a natural feeling for geometrical forms which never inhibited her from giving free play to her creativity. Bookbinding gave her a wide variety of possible compositions. On the inner side of the binding for *Pâques* she gummed brightly coloured squares, boldly anticipating the neo-plasticist paintings which were to come.

None of these collages were created from materials chosen at random. Sonia made a careful choice from among the many exotically coloured papers that could be obtained in those days. To these she added pieces of cloth, ribbons and even fragments of leather. Some of these bindings are entirely made out of material, such as the one executed for *Les Transplantés* by Canudo. With a little piece of green rep, or a scrap of woollen material, she could achieve an effect of glossy or matt velvet, or of crimson watered silk.

There is also a toy-box, of the same period, decorated with abstract designs. With this Robert and Sonia Delaunay discovered that rhythm, light and colour can pervade all the familiar forms of everyday life, even down to the smallest object. 'This box, exhibited at the Herbstsalon in Berlin in 1913, is particularly significant in that it is a familiar object, a homely object — but in Cubist style,' writes Jean Cassou. Here again, as in the bindings of the same period, Sonia Delaunay shows her desire to break with the conventional framework and techniques of painting. Both the exhibition at the Herbstsalon, and that which followed, organized by Herwarth Walden at the *Der Sturm* gallery, where a whole room was given over to the Delaunays' work, were to have a decisive influence on Expressionists such as Marc, Macke and even Paul Klee.

One last collage brings this period to a close: *Simultaneous Solar Prisms*. It surprises one by its melancholy. In contrast with the radiant colours which Sonia generally used, here we have — against a background of grey tissue paper — coloured papers, tinted with pastels and water-colours, that outline a diagonal movement arrested in full flight, like a single bar of an interrupted melody.

A few months later the war broke out and Sonia cut short her experimenting. It was the end of the collage period, except for one last time in Spain, where, inspired by Nijinsky, she made a kind of cushion in applique work. A new period was about to begin.

Philomène. Paris, 1907. Oil on canvas. 92 × 54.5 cm; no. 100.

55

Study for Philomène. Paris, 1907. Oil on canvas. 53.5 × 46 cm; no. 102. Musée National d'Art Moderne, Paris.

Portrait of the Russian poet Tchouïko, Paris, 1908. Oil on canvas. 55 × 46 cm; no. 19.

Young Girl Sleeping. Paris, 1907. Oil on canvas. 46 × 55 cm; no. 21. Musée National d'Art Moderne, Paris.

Young Finnish Girl. Finland, 1908. Oil on canvas. 80 × 64 cm; no. 2. Musée National d'Art Moderne, Paris

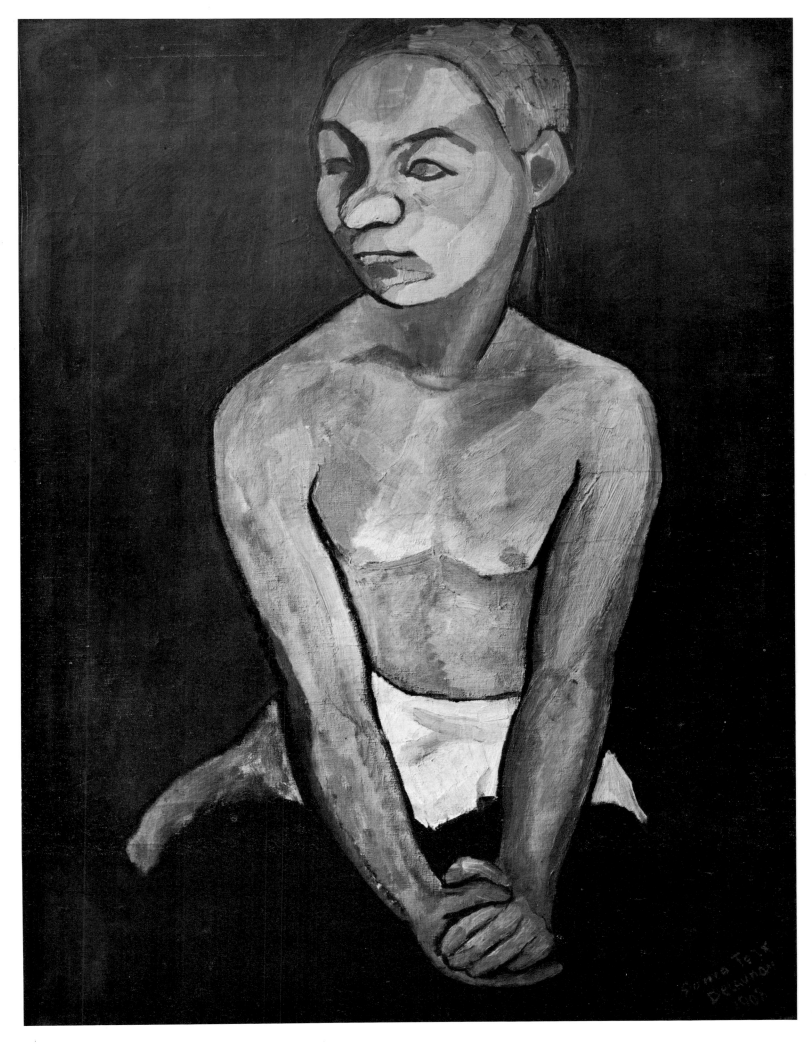

Yellow Nude. Paris, 1907. Oil on canvas. 64.5 × 98 cm; no. 1405.

Young Italian Woman.
Paris, 1907. Oil on canvas, 89 × 35 cm; no. 1.
Musée National d'Art Moderne, Paris.

Portrait of Mme Minsky. 1907. Oil on canvas. 55 × 46 cm; no. 1074.

Embroidery, Foliage. Paris, 1909. Wool on canvas. 85 × 60 cm; no. 548. Musée National d'Art Moderne, Paris.

Still-life. Paris, 1909
Watercolour on paper
49.5 × 38.8 cm; no. 74
Musée National d'Art
Moderne, Paris

Sonia and Wilhelm Uhde in their flat, Quai de la Tournelle, Paris, 1909;
on the walls, paintings by their artist friends.

Wilhelm Uhde by Robert Delaunay. 1907.
Oil on canvas. 80 × 64 cm.

Postcards: The Eiffel Tower at the turn of the century.

The Ile Saint-Louis, 1906. Drypoint etching. 25 × 32 cm.
Delaunay's first print; very few impressions printed.

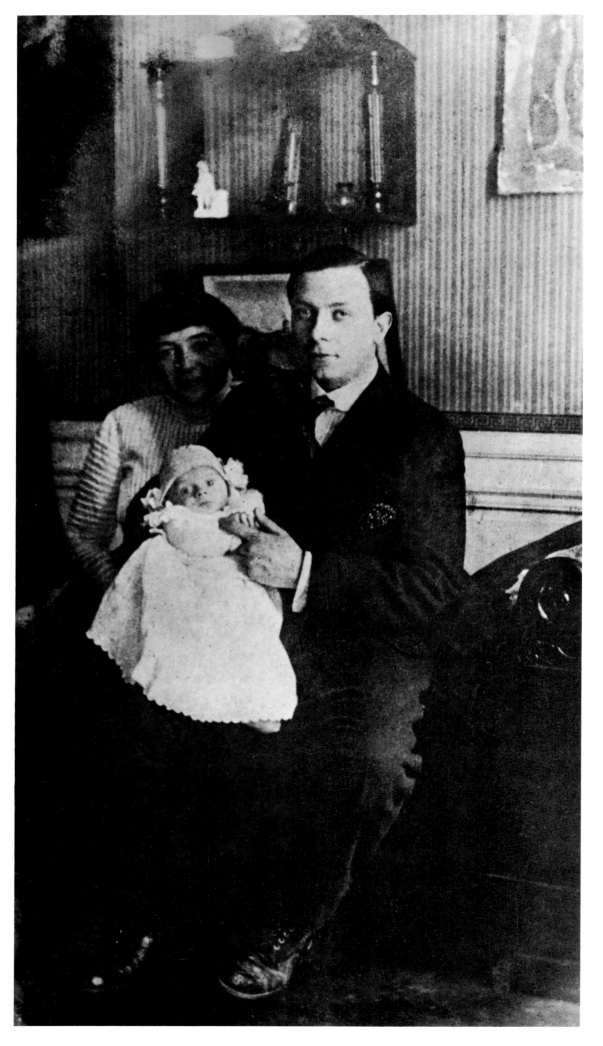

Robert and Sonia Delaunay
with their son Charles.
Taken in their studio,
Rue des Grands-Augustins, 1911.

Patchwork blanket made by
Sonia Delaunay for her son Charles's
cot. This work, inspired by Russian
peasant art, represents a decisive
moment in her progress towards
abstraction. The play of colours and
of geometrical patterns foreshadows
her later paintings.
Paris, 1911. 1.0 × 0.81 m.
Musée National d'Art Moderne, Paris.

Light study, Boulevard Saint-Michel.
Paris, 1912-1913. Crayon on ruled paper. 16.5 × 20.8 cm; no. 205.

Crowd study, Boulevard Saint-Michel
Paris, 1912. 16.5 × 21 cm; no. 206. Musée National d'Art Moderne, Paris

Light study, Boulevard Saint-Michel
Paris, 1912. Crayon on paper. 16.5 × 20.9 cm; no. 208
Musée National d'Art Moderne, Paris

Overleaf.

Crowd movement (Electric Prisms).
Paris, 1914. 25 × 19 cm; no. 47. Kunsthalle, Bielefeld.

Tango-Magic-City. Sketch.
Paris, 1913. Oil on canvas. 25 × 19 cm; no.50. Kunsthalle, Bielefeld.

Bal Bullier.
Paris, 1913. Oil on mattress ticking. 0.97 × 3.90 m; no. 52.
Musée National d'Art Moderne, Paris.

This work is important as much for its own merits as for the role which it played in
the development of the artist. She painted three other versions of the same theme.
In 1913, the Bal Bullier was one of the fashionable night spots of Montparnasse,
right opposite a well-known restaurant, the Closerie des Lilas. People came there to dance
the tango, which at the time was considered scandalous. Instead of an impressionist rendering
of the dance, as in Renoir and Degas—where the artist remains an observer—here we have
an attempt at transmitting the subjective impression of the dancer himself, lost in a turmoil
of noise and movement. The influence of both Gauguin's use of large expanses of colour and
the blurriness of early cinematography can be felt. We are confronted, in this vast modern mural,
with an effort to find an entirely original answer to a problem which the Quattrocento had also
sought to solve: how to represent movement and thereby break the immobility of a wall.

Bal Bullier.
Paris, 1913. Oil on canvas. 97 × 130 cm. Kunsthalle, Bielefeld.

In this other study, the attempt at representation of
dancing figures has disappeared. Only movement and
light are rendered through an intricate play of forms.

Première Robe Simultanée · Première robe simultanée

Sur la Robe, elle a un corps

Le corps de la femme est aussi bosselé que mon crâne

Glorieuse si tu es incarnée à l'esprit

Les couturiers font un sot métier

Autant que la phrénologie

Toilette appliquée, convenance, éducation

Tes yeux sont des kilos qui pèsent tous

la sensualité des femmes.

Tout ce qui fait bosse avance dans la profondeur

Les étoiles creusent le ciel

Et les couleurs déshabillent pas

contraste Madame

Madame

d'ai lu votre portrait ?

« Sur la robe elle a un corps »

Sous les plis, des bougies

Mare lumineuse et araignées petilles

Quand les corps se dévorent dans le dos avec

les omoplates au fond toutes

Tes seins terribles accouplés

Le ventre un disque qui bouge

Les seins que tes seins qui passe sous le pont d'Alexandre

Vente bougent à travers tes vertus

Soleil

Et les cris perpendiculaires des couleurs

tombent sur les cuisses des

Eau des St. Michel

Il y a dans les boto, tous les gens

Manuscript of Blaise Cendrars' poem 'Robe simultanée', inspired
by Sonia Delaunay's first dress in the genre in 1914.

Sonia Delaunay wearing the 'simultaneous dress',
at the Bal Bullier.

THE SIMULTANEOUS DRESS

To Madame Sonia Delaunay

On her dress she wears a body.
Woman's body is as bumpy as my skull
Glorious if you are made flesh
With Spirit.
Couturiers have a foolish profession
As foolish as phrenology
My eyes are kilos weighing the sensuality of women.
All things that swell advance in depth
The stars hollow out the sky.
Colours disrobe by contrast.
'On her dress she wears a body.'

Under the heather's arm
lurk shades of lunula and pistils
When the waters swirl down the back over sea-green shoulder blades
And the double conch of the breasts passes beneath the bridge of
                                                        [the rainbow

Belly
Discs
Sun
And the perpendicular cries of colours fall on the thighs
Sword of Saint Michael
There are hands stretching out
The drapes conceal the trick — all the eyes, all the flourishes and
                                all the habits of the Bal Bullier
And on the hip
The poet's signature.

BLAISE CENDRARS   1914

79

Postcard: Parisian women wearing hobble-skirt dresses, the autumn fashion in 1913.

1912 in the Valley of Chevreuse. Sonia Delaunay is
second from the right, with her
son in his pushchair. The
women are still
bundled up in conventional styles.

Dancer.
Paris, 1923.
Watercolour on paper.
37 × 26 cm; no. 66.

Electric Prisms. Paris, 1914. Crayon sketch. 24.5 × 21.5 cm; no. 841.

Electric Prisms.
Paris, 1914.
Oil on canvas. 250 × 250 cm; no. 36.
Musée National d'Art Moderne, Paris.

This square canvas, painted for the Salon des Indépendants of 1914, is, with
the *Bal Bullier*, one of the last major works of the period preceding the First World War.
It is born out of the observation of vibrating haloes of colour surrounding electric bulbs,
first noted by Blaise Cendrars in his 'Dix-neuf poèmes électriques'. Research into
the decomposition of light had reached a very advanced stage.

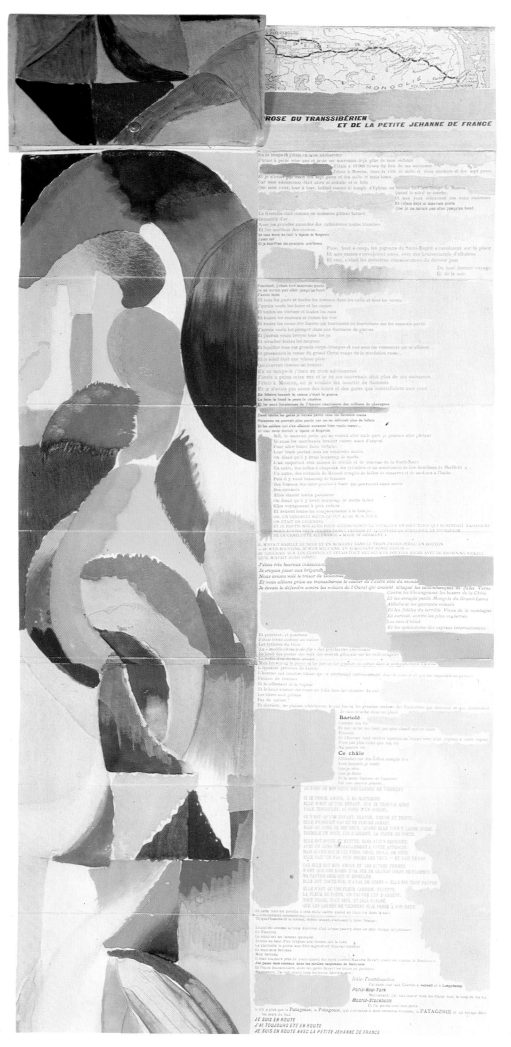

Prose du Transsibérien
et de la petite Jehanne de France.
Detail.

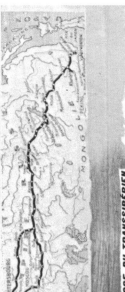

BLAISE CENDRARS

La Prose du Transsibérien
et de la Petite Jehanne de France

Couleurs simultanées de Mme DELAUNAY-TERK

TIRAGE DE LUXE Nº

De 1 à 8 pour les exemplaires parcheminés
De 9 à 36 pour les exemplaires japon
De 37 à 150 pour les exemplaires vieux japon

EDITIONS
HOMMES NOUVEAUX
4, rue de Savoie, 4
PARIS
1913

PROSE DU TRANSSIBÉRIEN ET D

REPRESENTATIO

PEINTURE Simultane

Mme De la unay-Terk B

Advertising leaflet for the *Prose du Transsibérien et de la petite Jéhanne de France.*

J'ai peur

Je ne sais pas aller jusqu'au bout

Comme mon ami Chagall je pourrais faire une série de tableaux déments
Mais je n'ai pas pris de notes en voyage

« Pardonnez-moi mon ignorance
« Pardonnez-moi de ne plus connaître l'ancien jeu des vers »

Tout ce qui concerne la guerre on peut le lire dans les *Mémoires* de Kouropatkine
Ou dans les journaux japonais qui sont aussi cruellement illustrés
A quoi bon me documenter
Je m'abandonne
Aux sursauts de ma mémoire.

A partir d'Irkoutsk le voyage devint beaucoup trop lent
Beaucoup trop long
Nous étions dans le premier train qui contournait le lac Baïkal
On avait orné la locomotive de drapeaux et de lampions
Et nous avions quitté la gare aux accents tristes de l'hymne au Tsar.
Si j'étais peintre je déverserais beaucoup de rouge, beaucoup de jaune sur la fin de ce voyage
Car je crois bien que nous étions tous un peu fous
Et qu'un délire immense ensanglantait les faces énervées de mes compagnons de voyage
Comme nous approchions de la Mongolie
Qui ronflait comme un incendie.
Le train avait ralenti son allure
Et je percevais dans le grincement perpétuel des roues
Les accents fous et les sanglots
D'une éternelle liturgie

J'ai vu
J'ai vu les trains silencieux les trains noirs qui revenaient de l'Extrême-Orient et qui passaient en fantômes
Et mon œil, comme le fanal d'arrière, court encore derrière ces trains
À Talga 100.000 blessés agonisaient faute de soins
J'ai visité les hôpitaux de Krasnoïarsk
Et à Khilok nous avons croisé un long convoi de soldats fous
J'ai vu dans les lazarets des plaies béantes des blessures qui saignaient à pleine orgue
Et les membres amputés dansaient autour ou s'envolaient dans l'air rauque
L'incendie était sur toutes les faces dans tous les cœurs
Des doigts idiots tambourinaient sur toutes les vitres
Et sous la pression de la peur les regards crevaient comme des abcès
Dans toutes les gares on brûlait tous les wagons
Et j'ai vu
J'ai vu des trains de 60 locomotives qui s'enfuyaient à toute vapeur pourchassées par les horizons en rut et des bandes de corbeaux qui s'envolaient désespérément après
Disparaître
Dans la direction de ...

Les trains d'Europe sont à quatre temps tandis que ceux d'Asie sont à cinq ou sept temps
D'autres vont en sourdine sont des berceuses
Et il y en a qui dans le bout monotone des roues me rappellent la prose lourde de Maeterlinck
J'ai déchiffré tous les textes confus des roues et j'ai rassemblé les éléments épars d'une beauté violente
Que je possède
Et qui me force.

Tsitsika et Kharbine
Je ne vais pas plus loin
C'est la dernière station
Je débarquai à Kharbine comme on venait de mettre le feu aux bureaux de la Croix-Rouge

O Paris

O Paris

Et les soldats qui l'égorgèrent
Et les galères
Et les vaisseaux
Et les engins prodigieux qu'ils inventa
Et toutes les tueries
L'histoire antique
L'histoire moderne
Les tourbillons
Les naufrages

Même celui du Titanic que j'ai lu dans le journal
Autant d'images associatives que je ne peux pas développer dans mes vers
Car je suis encore fort mauvais poète
Car l'univers me déborde
Car j'ai négligé de m'assurer contre les accidents de chemin de fer
Car je ne sais pas aller jusqu'au bout
Et j'ai peur.

Paris
Ville de la Tour unique du grand Gibet et de la Roue

Hier matin
Ivan Oulitch avait les cheveux blancs
Et Kolia Nicolaï Ivanovitch se ronge les doigts depuis trois jours...
Fais comme elles la Mort la Famine fais ton métier
Ça coûte cent sous, en transsibérien ça coûte cent roubles
Enfièvre les banquettes et rougeoie sous la table
Le diable est au piano
Ses doigts noueux excitent toutes les femmes
La Nature
Les Gouges
Fais ton métier
Jusqu'à Kharbine...

— Dis Blaise, sommes-nous bien loin de Montmartre ?

Non mais... fiche-moi la paix... laisse-moi tranquille
Tu as les hanches angulaires
Ton ventre est aigre et tu as la chaude-pisse

C'est tout ce que Paris a mis dans ton giron
C'est aussi un peu d'âme... car tu es malheureuse
J'ai pitié j'ai pitié *viens vers moi sur mon cœur*
Les roues sont les moulins à vent du pays de Cocagne

Et les moulins à vent sont les béquilles qu'un mendiant fait tournoyer

Nous sommes les culs-de-jatte de l'espace
Nous roulons sur nos quatre plaies
On nous a rogné les ailes
Les ailes de nos sept péchés
Et tous les trains sont les bilboquets du diable
Basse-cour
Le monde moderne
La vitesse n'y peut mais
Le monde moderne
Les lointains sont par trop loin

Et au bout du voyage c'est terrible d'être un homme avec une femme

« Blaise, dis, sommes-nous bien loin de Montmartre ? »

Que pitié J'ai pitié viens vers moi je vais te conter une histoire
Viens dans mon lit
Viens sur mon cœur
Je vais te conter une histoire

Oh viens ! viens !

Aux Fidji règne l'éternel printemps
La paresse
Viens dans les Iles perdues du Pacifique !
Elles ont nom du Phénix, des Marquises
Bornéo et Java
Et Célèbes à la forme d'un chat
Nous ne pouvons pas aller au Japon
Viens au Mexique !
Sur ses hauts plateaux les tulipiers fleurissent
Les lianes tentaculaires sont la chevelure du soleil
On dirait la palette et les pinceaux d'un peintre
Des couleurs étourdissantes comme des gongs,
Rousseau y a été
Il y a ébloui sa vie
C'est le pays des oiseaux
L'oiseau du paradis l'oiseau-lyre
Le toucan l'oiseau moqueur
Et le colibri niche au cœur des lys noirs

Viens !
Nous nous aimerons dans les ruines majestueuses d'un temple aztèque
Tu seras mon idole
Une idole bariolée enfantine un peu laide et bizarrement étrange
Oh viens !

L'amour plane dans l'herbe haute et la chaude syphilis rôde sous les bananiers

Si tu veux nous irons en aéroplane et nous survolerons le pays des mille lacs,
Les nuits y sont démesurément longues
L'ancêtre préhistorique aura peur de mon moteur
J'atterrirai
Et je construirai un hangar pour mon avion avec les os fossiles de mammouths
Le feu primitif réchauffera notre pauvre amour
Samovar
Et nous nous aimerons bien bourgeoisement près du pôle
Oh viens !

Jeanne JEANNETTE Ninette nini ninon nichon
Mimi mamour ma poupette mon Pérou
Dodo dondon
Carotte ma crotte
Chouchou p'tit-cœur
Cocotte
Chérie p'tite-chèvre
Mon p'tit-péché mignon
Concon
Coucou
Elle dort

Elle dort
Et de toutes les heures du monde elle n'en a pas gobé une seule
Tous les visages entrevus dans les gares
Toutes les horloges
L'heure de Paris l'heure de Berlin l'heure de Saint-Pétersbourg et l'heure de toutes les gares
Et à Oufa, le visage ensanglanté du canonnier
Et le cadran bêtement lumineux de Grodno
Et l'avance perpétuelle du train
Tous les matins on met les montres à l'heure
Le train avance et le soleil retarde
Rien n'y fait, j'entends les cloches sonores
Le gros bourdon de Notre-Dame
La cloche aigrelette du Louvre qui sonna la Barthélemy
Les carillons rouillés de Bruges-la-Morte
Les sonneries électriques de la bibliothèque de New-York

Les campanes de Venise
Et les cloches de Moscou, l'horloge de la Porte-Rouge qui me comptait les heures quand j'étais dans un bureau
Et mes souvenirs
Le train tonne sur les plaques tournantes
Le train roule
Un gramophone grasseye une marche tzigane
Et le monde, comme l'horloge du quartier juif de Prague tourne éperdûment à rebours.
Effeuille la rose des vents
Voici que bruissent les orages déchaînés
Les trains roulent en tourbillon sur les réseaux enchevêtrés
Bilboquets diaboliques
Il y a des trains qui ne se rencontrent jamais
D'autres se perdent en route
Les chefs de gare jouent aux échecs

Tric-trac
Billard
Caramboles
PARABOLES
La voie ferrée est une nouvelle géométrie
SYRACUSE

PRISME SOLAIRE SIMULTANE

multaneous Solar Prism
Woman with Sunshade).
aris, 1914. *Pochoir.*
9 × 22 cm; no. 891.

Solar Prism
(Woman with Sunshade).
Paris. 1913-1914.
Paper pasted on cardboard.
28.5 × 21 cm; no. 35.
othschild Collection, New York.

The Iberian Period

'Dis, Blaise, sommes-nous loin de Montmartre?' (Tell me, Blaise, are we far from Montmartre?) sang the young Jehanne de France, in Cendrars's poem. Alas yes, for the war had scattered friends far and wide. Blaise was in Champagne; Apollinaire had joined up too; and the Delaunays were in Portugal. At the outbreak of war they were on holiday in Spain. There seemed no reason for returning to France, since Robert was not likely to be called up, having been discharged as unfit from the army in 1908.

The Delaunays remained in Spain and Portugal from 1914 till 1920. They spent the winter of 1915-16 in Madrid, and from there they moved to Villa do Conde, near Oporto in Northern Portugal, then to Monçao in the Minho valley; finally they went to Vigo, just across the border in Spain. Sonia's major compositions of this period, the *Markets in the Minho,* were painted at Villa do Conde. These, with the *Bal Bullier* (1913) and the *Electric Prisms* (1914) are her essential contribution to Orphism; this was a period of tremendous creative and decorative activity for Sonia Delaunay.

The peninsular sun fed her exuberant lyricism. Sun, light, and the colourful peasant life (reminding her of her native Russia) gave her new means of expression and inspired her to return to representation. The fiestas, the markets, the lively streets, the fruit stalls, were one and all translated by the artist into plastic forms and used to show her new vision of the world. Certain paintings — for example the *Little Girl with Watermelons* (1915) — demonstrate how she derived pictorial components — coloured discs, luminous rainbow segments — from reality.

Inspired by the quality of light, as well as the local life in Portugal, Sonia set about pursuing the researches on which she had embarked in Paris. Robert Delaunay remarked in a note-book that the rays of the sun seemed to them more tangible, more human, 'than the cold transparent light of Madrid'. And he added: 'From the moment one arrives one feels bathed in an atmosphere of dream and somnolence. The rhythmic indifference of oxen with their great horns and old-fashioned yokes, a tiny girl wrapped in vast multi-coloured shawls at their side. Sight upon sight, disturbing by their very singularity, succeed one another. Violent colour contrasts, women's dresses, bright shawls against the sharp metallic green of watermelons. Markets in the sun, women hidden behind heaps of pumpkins and other vege-tables, while tall figures go by bearing on their heads vases, irregular and pure in form like antique jars. Traditional peasant dress, an intoxicating wealth of colour. . . . Interspersed among the dazzling fullness of these forms, the resonant black and sparkling white of the men's costumes bring a touch of solemnity and angularity into this moving sea of colours.'

To this Portuguese period belongs the vast composition *Homage to the Donor* which was intended for the façade of the Valença do Minho convent, as well as several *Still-lifes, Portuguese Women, Self-portraits* in tempera or gouache, the *Flamencos* and designs for 'simultaneous' dresses — whilst Delaunay painted a series of *Still-lifes, Coffee-pots,* and *Portuguese Women* as well. Both of them took advantage of the enormous studios they had in the unfinished Valença do Minho convent to paint large-scale canvases.

Of all the works they did, the *Market in the Minho* is the best; it is a climax of denseness and discipline of composition, at-tempting to define reality through a complex interplay of repre-sentational and abstract coloured elements. The aim is not, of course, to represent a scene, but, by decomposing and recomposing it, to make a study of light in the Minho valley. There exist two versions of this work — one finished, which is of medium size, and one large-scale — as well as many preliminary sketches and studies of detail. In the final version, the coloured discs generate forms and movements and, although they appear on a single vertical plane, create a space composed of interrupted concentric strips varying in size and number. The composition, set diagonally from left to right, converges on a focal point of colour and dynamism situated at the level of the faces of the women with watermelons. In the foreground, the crowds form a descending line which comes to a reluctant halt in front of the open arcs of the fruit and vegetable stalls in the lower right-hand corner. The arcades of the viaduct, the silhouettes of the young girl with the stick and the oxen depicted full-face, are the only representational elements in the painting. Their purpose is to counteract and stabilize the tangle of circles, slowing down the rhythm and creating an 'atmosphere of somnolence'. In the upper left-hand corner, a checker-board of rectangles suggests distant roofs and façades. As for the colours, the dominant reds, oranges, ochres and yellows contribute warmth of tone; most of the greens have been mingled with yellows. Each colour increases in intensity by contact with its complementary and by the interplay of simultaneous contrasts; dissonant tones accentuate forms, making them vibrate. In certain sketches, the points of concentration, the major 'discs' and the 'static' figurative elements — if not yet fully expressed — are well placed, and the choice of colours is already made.

Once the first version was completed, Sonia Delaunay began

on the second, which she intended to be colossal. It is the master-piece of the series, one of the most electric and visionary creations of Orphism. She used the same elements, but they were infused with a new power; the discs increased in number, subdivided into concentric rings, widened out into haloes. Freed from the closed-in loops which circumscribed the composition of the first version, the rhythm soared upwards, extending beyond the very frame of the canvas. The central figure became tall and willowy.

Studies and sketches enable us to follow the creative process step by step. One sees that the main discs and the arches of the viaduct were painted first. Initially geometrical, the circles were then worked on to give them dynamic impact; they were some-times broken down as in the right-hand foreground — this corner seems to have been studied particularly carefully. The figurative forms appeared later: the seated woman, the bust of the young girl (which reminds us of the Finnish girls drawn earlier), the head of the ox with its long horns, a few houses. More sketches paved the way from the smaller to the larger version. Circles appeared, the central area acquired flexibility, a new 'core' deve-loped in the top right hand corner. But the seated vegetable seller had not yet been introduced into the composition.

In her own words, Sonia Delaunay describes her arrival at Villa do Conde: 'A world apart, houses of shimmering whiteness against a distant ultramarine blue ocean. Codfish laid out to dry everywhere. On the right, a castle and a viaduct perched on a hill. Inland, the fields dotted with oxen, and silhouettes of women standing like biblical figures. My first sweeping impres-sion. Then each detail struck me: colours of shawls, women's clothing, tanned skins, dark green watermelons with deep red hearts paling into pink, and all bathed in blinding sunlight. I felt drunk with colour and immediately set about painting — as did Delaunay and our Portuguese artist friend, Eduardo Vianna. Our stay at Villa do Conde, in a house lost among dunes with flowering cacti in the garden, was like a fairy tale.'

Fearing their own tendency to intellectualism, and, from the moment they arrived in the Iberian peninsula, finding in Nature sufficient inspiration, the Delaunays abandoned the purely abstract treatment of forms and colours. Their environment seemed to call for a certain degree of representation, and, as an example, of the fourteen more or less elaborated sketches we possess for the *Markets in the Minho,* all are more or less figurative, representing mainly fruit and vegetable sellers (pumpkins and watermelons are a blessing to an artist working with circular forms!).

Sonia Delaunay did not return to abstraction until 1920, when she used it in her printed materials; as for Robert, he abandoned it until after 1930.

As early as 1912, the Delaunays had figured among the avant-garde of abstract art. Robert Delaunay's famous 'simultaneous' *Window* series, eulogized by Apollinaire, had had a notable impact on such young artists as Marc and Macke in Germany, and Bruce, Frost, Macdonald, Wright and Russell in America. Paul Klee wrote an enthusiastic article on one of the *Windows* exhibited at the Zurich Museum in 1912, and translated Delaunay's notes on the phenomenon of light for *Der Sturm* at the beginning of 1913. Klee himself then worked on similar lines ('Abstract: coloured circles linked by coloured strips') and carried out experi- 99 ments under the Kairwan sun analogous to Delaunay's in Portugal.

A collaborator rather than a disciple, Sonia joined her husband in the study of laws of contrasts and 'simultaneous' discs. They considered that the disc was the form which least restricts colour, and at the same time contributes a maximum of dynamism to a composition; from then on they made extensive use of this technique. The markets of the Minho valley gave Sonia the opportunity to apply with great originality the laws she and her husband had elaborated.

In 1926, she explained: 'Chevreul had discovered these laws scientifically and had checked them experimentally; but in Spain and Portugal, where the radiancy of light is greater and purer than here, my husband and I were able to confirm them in nature itself. The very quality of this light enabled us to go further than he had in analysing harmonies obtained through contrasts, and even to discover dissonances: I mean rapid vibrations caused by the proximity of warm and cold tones which stimulate an intense excitement through colour.'

Two other major works — major both in scale and in artistic content — were done during this first Portuguese period. We are referring to the *Flamencos* painted at Valença do Minho in 1916. It was during this time that she also worked on cover designs for the magazine *Vogue*. They returned once more to Portugal before leaving finally for Barcelona and Madrid.

The *Large Flamenco* (which was exhibited at the London Royal Academy in 1969) is a much more abstract composition than the *Small Flamenco*. The composition as a whole already gives the characteristic illusion of infinite rhythm. The face of the woman

Market in the Minho. Portugal, 1915. Wax crayon on backed paper. 73 × 92 cm; no. 842. Musée d'Art et d'Histoire, Geneva.

is the only truly figurative detail of the painting. The discs representing the breasts bring to mind Cendrars' poem 'La Robe simultanée' (p. 79), and the same idea reappeared in the costume designs for *Cléopâtre*. To set the context, she introduced lettering in the top right-hand corner, as she had already done in the *Electric Prisms* (1914). The great circular ribbons widen out from an almost perfectly centred point just below the male singer. The latter — with the lower portion of the painting — is the least colourful part of the composition, a shadowy, ghostly figure.

The *Small Flamenco* is far more representational and Expressionist in inspiration. The colourful bust of the woman is strongly painted in; the guitar, though not at all reminiscent of a Cubist instrument, is treated in two distinct ways, the upper portion being realistic and the lower portion composed of discs. Although this version does not soar to the lyrical heights of the *Large Flamenco*, it is nevertheless, in its expressive power, a work of great quality. The two heads are not very different from those which were painted later by Alexej Jawlensky, certain German Expressionists, Francis Bacon and even Chaim Soutine. In both compositions, the singer or dancer stands out in brilliant colours in the left foreground, and the accompanist remains in the shadows, as in a live show. If the large circular forms and discs already evoke the music of Andalusian songs, the entirely abstract gouache, *Flamenco Singers* of 1916 is a pure transposition of musical rhythms into form and colour.

In Madrid, Sonia Delaunay slowly returned to social life and tackled new tasks, such as the famous costumes for Diaghilev's ballets. She took part in various artistic exhibitions. One of the last, held at the Salón Mateu in January 1921, incited Robert

Delaunay to write: 'Sonia Delaunay transformed the Salón Mateu into a fantastic pageantry of light, colour and rhythmical form.... In the middle of cubes and greyness, appeared the first rainbow, heralding new circular forms. Few could appreciate it, for France still laughed at the Douanier Rousseau!'

In 1917, on the Rambla in Barcelona, the first news of the Russian Revolution reached Sonia Delaunay. This meant financial ruin, but she and Robert wept for joy.

In Madrid in 1918, they received one of Tristan Tzara's Dada Manifestos. Excitedly, the Delaunays realized that the ideas formulated in the manifesto corresponded to their own, and that soon things would start moving again in Paris. They began to think of returning.

Portugal, 1914-1917: a street in Oporto; a cart entering Oporto; northern peasant costume.

Still-life. Madrid, 1915. Wax on canvas. 84 cm diameter; no. 884. Morse Collection, New York.

Postcards of Portugal: Peasant street procession near Oporto;
peasant woman from Oporto area.

Woman at the Market (Watermelon Woman). Portugal, 1915. Oil on canvas. 79 × 96 cm; no. 5. S. Benador Collection, Geneva.

108

Market in the Minho.
Portugal, 1915.
Wax on canvas. 197 × 216 cm; no. 57.
Musée National d'Art Moderne, Paris.

This work and its numerous preparatory sketches have been analysed by Charles Goerg in his essay *Le Marché au Minho de Sonia Delaunay*, Geneva, 1965.

Market. Study from Nature. Portugal, 1916. Wax on canvas. 113 × 140 cm; no. 563.

Little Girl with Watermelons. Portugal, 1915. Pasted on canvas. 45 × 60.5 cm; no. 26. Musée Saint-Pierre, Lyon.

Portuguese Still-life. Portugal, 1916. Wax on canvas. 38 × 56 cm; no. 863. Georges Pompidou Collection, Paris.

Preliminary design for *Homage to the Donor*.
Portugal, 1916. Wax on canvas. 130 × 326 cm; no. 565.
Musée National d'Art Moderne, Paris.

There exist four versions of this work, one of which is in
the Museum of Monumental Art at Lund. Political unrest
in Portugal prevented the completion of this work, which
was intended for the Jesuit church of Valença do Minho.

Group of Portuguese Women. Sketch for detail of *Homage to the Donor*
Portugal, 1916. No 464. Private collection, Seattle

Flamenco Singer (Small Flamenco). Madrid, 1915. Distemper, oil and wax on canvas. 91 × 91 cm; no. 6.

Flamenco Singer (Large Flamenco). Madrid, 1916. Wax on canvas. 174 × 144 cm; no. 145

Sonia Delaunay painting the final version of the
Market in the Minho at Villa do Conde. Portugal, 1916.

Portuguese Still-life.
Portugal 1915. Glue on paper. 62.5 × 47 cm; no. 158.
Private collection, Los Angeles.

Dancer.
Portugal, 1916. Watercolour and gouache on paper. 36 × 23 cm; no. 416.
Musée National d'Art Moderne, Paris.

Dancer
Vigo, 1917. Watercolour on paper. 35.5 × 25.5 cm; no. 875
Private collection, Paris

120

Sonia Delaunay-Terk 1917

Disc. Portugal, 1915. Wax on paper. 19.7 × 14 cm; no. 153.

Portugal, 1915: painted pottery, watercolours, material with local Portuguese designs; in the background, on the right the poster for Cendrars' poem *Zénith*, on the left a gouache, *Portuguese Toys*.

№ 154

Disc. Portugal, 1916. Wax on paper. 26.4 × 20.5 cm; no. 154.

125

'Simultaneous' dress. Portugal, 1917. Watercolour on paper. 35 × 24.9 cm; no. 446. Private collection, London.

126

'Simultaneous' costume. Portugal, 1916. Watercolour on paper. 25 × 17 cm; no. 407. Gimpel Collection, London.

Dancer. Vigo, 1917. Gouache and crayon on paper; 47 × 34.5 cm; no. 462. Musée National d'Art Moderne, Paris.

Sonia Delaunay-Terk
Costume, porté par
Gaby
au Petit Casino
Madrid 1919

Costume worn by Gaby. Madrid, 1919. Indian ink on paper. 23.5 × 18 cm; no. 566.

Theatre and Fashion

Theatre Costumes

In 1918, Serge de Diaghilev, then in Madrid, decided to revive his ballet *Cléopâtre*. As he had become a great friend of the Delaunays, he commissioned new costumes from Sonia and new stage sets from Robert — the original costumes and decor designed by Bakst having been destroyed in a fire during their South American tour.

Based on a short story by Théophile Gautier, the ballet had originally been created in 1909. It staged a Cleopatra, prepared to die at dawn, seeking a lover for one night. With Fokine's orchestration, it became more than a pantomime, it was a real tragedy expressed by dance, with the choir transformed into a corps de ballet and the words conveyed through gesture. It was a new way to tell a story, letting it unfold with only dramatic expression, colours and the music of Arensky, Rimsky-Korsakov, Glinka, Mussorgsky and Glazunov as supports. The faces of the dancers were required to transmit suffering and desire. In the 1909 production, Nijinsky had danced the young soldier, Karsavina the young slave girl; and the role of Cleopatra had been mimed, not danced, by Ida Rubinstein. In 1918 the principal roles were danced by Massine and Tchernicheva. Sonia Delaunay had conceived a mummy-like Cleopatra entwined in lengths of material, each one different from the other; these scarves were unwound little by little as the plot unfolded. Once unwrapped, Cleopatra was revealed in a fabulous costume designed to make the audience gasp with admiration. This took place against a background representing a view of the Nile, designed by Robert Delaunay.

This was followed in 1919 by the decoration of the 'Petit Casino' in Madrid, and the design of clothes for Gaby, who was the star there at the time. Sonia then undertook to design the opera-singer Lahovska's costumes for *Aïda,* to be produced at the Barcelona Opera House. The singer had written to her 'This opera is so old and well known that in order to listen to it with any attention (this being the only justifiable reason for its revival) it needs to be dressed up anew.' Back in Paris, Sonia Delaunay had many other opportunities to apply her talents to the theatre. The history of ballet and theatre can boast of few achievements that display such a wealth of imagination.

The Ballets Russes had proclaimed the triumph of colour and variegated materials even before the First World War. In 1917, at the Cabaret Voltaire in Zurich, the Dadaists had recited their poems in costumes which paralysed all movement. The same year saw the creation of *Parade,* the combined work of Erik Satie (music), Jean Cocteau (plot) and Picasso (costumes and decor). Picasso's costumes quite transformed the habitual conception of theatrical dress — each dancer had been turned into a moving piece of decor more than a dancer dancing. Encouraged by Jean Cocteau, Picasso had created costumes that were in fact 'sculpture-objects'. But Sonia Delaunay's costumes were still more original. With the exception of such outstanding realizations as Fernand Léger's designs for the Swedish Ballet in 1922, Yacouloff's *Pas d'acier* and Pevsner and Gabo's *La Chatte* in 1927, and Miró's *Les Jeux d'enfants* in 1932, few works can be said to have had such far-reaching an impact.

In 1923, Tscherez organized the *Soirée du cœur à barbe* to be held on 6 and 7 July at the Théâtre Michel, Rue des Mathurins. On the programme were works by Stravinsky, Darius Milhaud, Georges Auric and Erik Satie; a film by Man Ray, *Le Retour à la* 131 *raison*; an abstract film by Hans Richter; poems by Cocteau, Soupault, Tzara, Ribemont-Dessaignes, Apollinaire, Reverdy and many others; a dance by Madame Codreanu to music by Georges Auric with costumes designed by Sonia Delaunay. The notorious *Cœur à gaz* of Tristan Tzara was also on the programme. This three-act play had first been produced on 10 June 1921, at the Galerie Montaigne of the Théâtre des Champs-Elysées. For the 1923 production, Tzara had commissioned the costumes from Sonia Delaunay. Jacqueline Chaumont was to be the 'Mouth', Marcel Herrant the 'Eyebrow', René Crevel the 'Eye', Pierre de Massot the 'Nose'. Tzara indicated that the 'Neck' was to be below stage, the 'Nose' above and facing the audience; the other characters could walk in and out *ad lib.*; the 'Heart', gas-heated, was to walk around slowly. It was announced as the greatest three-act swindle of the century, which would bring luck only to industrialized fools who believed in geniuses. The actors were instructed to give the play the intensity of masterpieces like *Macbeth* and *Chantecler,* but to treat the author — who was no genius — with little respect and thereby assure the lack of serious-ness of a text which introduced no innovation into theatre tech-nique. Motionless navels replaced the eyes. The play did not bring Tzara much luck. It was shouted down by Breton's Sur-realists, and one only caught a glimpse of Grabovsky's stage sets and Sonia Delaunay's costumes. All the same it gave René Crevel, poet and novelist, his first chance to meet the Delaunays.

He wrote: 'A group of friends had come together to put on *Cœur à gaz.* One day, Tristan Tzara organized a rehearsal at the Delaunays'. From the moment I entered their flat, I was amazed. The walls were entirely covered with multi-coloured

132

poems. There was Georges Auric, a pot of paint in one hand, busy painting a splendid treble clef and notes; next to him, Pierre de Massot was writing some friendly inscription; the host himself was inviting all newcomers to set to work; others admired the grey crepe de chine curtain on which Sonia Delaunay had quite spontaneously embroidered, in large sweeping strokes, a poem by Philippe Soupault.

'High spirits and enthusiasm are very rare qualities, and when these are channelled intelligently, their value is beyond compare. A mere five minutes in Sonia Delaunay's house — and who cannot say he feels surer of himself, even happier? The reason is quite simple, at last a place where speeches, sententious phrases, the inevitable misleading discussions are not called for. . . . You walk in, Sonia immediately shows you her dresses, her furniture, her designs for other dresses and for other pieces of furniture. Nothing here resembles what you might have seen in fashion houses or at exhibitions. This is something truly new — and yet, the involuntary suspicion which usually accompanies the shock of total novelty is absent: it has been turned into optimism. You look at new things and you are carried away — they become unexpected fruits whose substance, form and colour can only sharpen your appetite, your curiosity.

'As you enter, the dining-room is on the left. This is Robert Delaunay's kingdom, firstly because eating is one of his greatest pleasures (Philippe Soupault even praised his appetite), then because he works there and keeps his paint pots there. The sitting-room faces the entrance; it was the sitting-room door that Georges Auric and Pierre de Massot were busy autographing the first time I came. I disturbed them pitilessly, and went into

Sonia's domain. At the time, she had not yet finished arranging it, indeed it would not even have crossed her mind to ask others help her look for materials and furniture. A creator herself, how could she ask a stranger to design her tables or her armchairs? Familiar, everyday objects are as poems to her, and she considers them quite as important as paintings . . .

'When I walked in, she was putting the finishing touches to the designs of the costumes we were to wear in *Cœur à gaz*. These were very simple — I nearly said 'perfectly reasonable'! What I mean is they had not been made in a random fashion, they were born pencil in hand so to speak, composed and complete. Indeed they had nothing in common with anything that had been thought up till then. Their straight-forward audacity was compelling. Once more this was proof that only spontaneous inspiration can be objective. To speak of immediate synthesis would be more accurate — furthermore, in each single creation she achieved a whole. There is colour, substance — but also muscle and bone. Her furniture has a framework, her dresses are a pretext to enhance the stature. Sonia dresses in the strongest sense of the word. . . . She creates, but what she creates is less a dress or a scarf than a new person.'

Sonia Delaunay herself writes of her stage work: 'The theatre of colour should be composed like a line of Mallarmé, like a page of Joyce. It should be a perfectly pure juxtaposition, a series of precise concatenations, each element gauged to its exact value. Beauty resides in the power of suggestion inciting the spectator's participation. Creation is incomplete without his contribution and spirit. Beauty refuses to bow to the limitations of meaning or description.'

In 1923 Sonia Delaunay was able to put her ideas into practice: in the *Dancers with Discs* which was organized by the poet Iliazd at the *Licorne*. Here, Madame Codreanu danced 'colour'. The means employed for the costume were basically simple. There were three elements, a large cardboard disc covered with several types of material of varying shades of orange and green, hid the face and bust of the dancer; a semi-circle in two shades of red and one of blue made up the short skirt; attached to her right hand was a black circle, and to her left hand a white one. By its very rigidity, the costume imposed its own law; unable to turn, the dancer was forced to discover colour contrasts in movement whilst remaining facing the audience. By subtly modifying the colour planes, Madame Codreanu was able to create a new syntax of colour which was beyond all description. Imagination reigned unfettered.

'This was my first venture in this line,' writes the artist, 'a trial run really. Had I had the opportunity to explore further, assuredly I would have found a way to develop my idea, to diversify the possibilities of expression and overcome the rigidity, perhaps even by using mechanical and electrical accessories. The song would then have become inexhaustible.'

On 23 February 1923, the association of Russian artists in Paris organized *Transmental,* a fancy-dress ball at the Bal Bullier, in aid of the artists' relief fund — the very Bal Bullier, 31 Avenue de l'Observatoire, where the Delaunays had spent many evenings before 1914. The programme speaks for itself: 'This is going to be a vast fun fair. There will be chariots, traffic jams, competitions to choose beauty queens, gigolos and gigolettes, bearded women, pigs' merry-go-rounds, fake massacres, a four-headed foetus, mermaids and mythological dances, and oddities made of flesh and unbreakable wire, which are at the same time fire-proof, insured against accidents and safe for children of all ages. Delaunay will be there with his Transatlantic troupe of pick-pockets, Goncharova with her boutique of masks, Larionov with his 'rayonism', Léger and his *orchestre-décor*, André Levinson and his all-star company, Marie Vassilieff and her babies, Tristan Tzara and his fat birds, Nina Peyne and her jazz band, Pascin and his original belly dancers, Codreanu with her choreography, Iliazd and his bouts of fever reaching a temperature of 106, and many other attractions. The ball-rooms will be decorated by the best artists of today.'

Already anticipating the boutique she was to create in 1925, Sonia Delaunay had set up her booth of fashions at the ball.

On Friday 14 March of the following year, there was another big ball at the Bullier, the *Bal banal* — once again in aid of the Russian artists' fund. The names of the best artists of the day figured on the bill, including quite naturally those of the Delaunays. The entrance tickets were designed by Goncharova, the poster by Picasso, the programme by Derain, Matisse, Braque, Brancusi, Bourdelle, Lhote, Foujita, Léger, Segonzac, Zadkine, Dufy and many others.

The programme comprised: *Triomphe du cubisme, tableau vivant,* direction and choreography by Larionov, costumes and stage set by Barthe; *Le Neveu de Vinci,* with the cooperation of Raphael; *Sans eau;* Paul Cézanne, *Salon des Indépendants,* Derain, *Pompeii,* Picasso, *Ballets russes,* Matisse, *De chez Bernheim,* Braque, *Valet du roy,* Metzinger, *La Rotonde,* Lhote, *De l'école primaire;* Lipschitz; Severini. 'If interested in other names, please consult Apollinaire's Cubist book at meetings no one goes to these days and at the auctions of the Hôtel Drouot.'

These were the golden days of the *années folles,* when for the Delaunays work and fun were the same.

It was at about this time that Joseph Delteil wrote his poem 'La Mode qui vient' (p. 167) and asked Sonia Delaunay to create multi-coloured costumes and 'simultaneous' materials for it. This poetic display was organized by the collector Laurent Monnier at Claridge's in Paris in honour of Marshal Foch. Naturally the press covered the event: 'Last Saturday, high society was to be seen at the pages' ball. Russian dancers, cossacks and peasants, opened the evening's entertainment; this was followed by a parade illustrating yesterday's, today's and tomorrow's fashions. The entrance of the latter was greeted with applause by the assembled company.' (25 May 1924.)

Sonia Delaunay had successfully blended wit and poetry in her costumes, and in 1926 she worked, with equal success, on the costumes for two films, Le Somptier's *Le p'tit parigot* and Marcel L'Herbier's *Vertige.*

She was also involved in several plays, designing for actresses like Gabrielle Dorziat, Lucienne Bogaert and Paulette Pax. In 1925 she designed sixteen different costumes for the Rio de Janeiro carnival. Each was completely original, though through them all ran the same vein of fantasy, which even today would still guarantee their success.

Cleopâtre 1918

S. Delaunay Terk

692

Costume designs for *Cléopâtre* for Diaghilev's Ballets Russes.
On the left, costume for Léonide Massine.
Madrid, 1918. Jacques Damase Collection, Paris.

INDICACIONES DE SERVICIO

Recibido de

Hilo núm.

El Oficial,

INDICACIONES EVENTUALES

Correo pagado............ P. P.
Respuesta pagada........ R. P.
Telegrama colacionado..... T. C.

Acuse de recibo.......... C. R.
Telegrama recomendado.... T. R.
Telegrama á hacer seguir... F. S.

Número

En los telegramas impresos en caracteres romanos por los agentes telegráficos, el primer número que figura, después del punto de origen, es el número de orden; el segundo indica el de palabras contadas; y los siguientes, la fecha, mes y hora del depósito.
El Estado no acepta responsabilidad alguna respecto del servicio de la Telegrafía.

núm.   Palabras   á las

DE LONDON 328 35 6 22/10 VBO

AVONS DEBUTE HIER AVEC INDESCRIPTIBLE SUCCES VOTRE DECOR PEENT PAR RUSSE WOLMARC ETAIT APPLAUDI
AU LEVEE DU RIDEAU COSTUME CLÉOPATRE ADMIRABLE AMITIES ET SOUVENIRS .= SERGE DIAGHILEW SAVOY HOTEL

From left to right: Robert Delaunay, Boris Kochno, Igor Stravinsky, Sonia Delaunay, Serge de Diaghilev, Manuel de Falla, and M. Barrochi. Madrid, 1918.

Telegram sent from Diaghilev in London to the Delaunays in Madrid after the successful first night of *Cléopâtre*.

141

Tchernichova as Cleopatra. Costume by Sonia Delaunay. Ballets Russes, Madrid, 1918.

Madame aga Lahovska
en "Amnéris" en Aïda

Sonia Delaunay-Terk
6/11 18
Madrid

693

René Crevel in *Le Cœur à gaz,* play by Tristan Tzara.
The performance at the Théâtre Michel was broken up by André Breton and his friends.

Four costumes for Joseph Delteil's poem *La Mode qui vient* (see p. 167), performed at the Hôtel Claridge, Paris, in 1923.

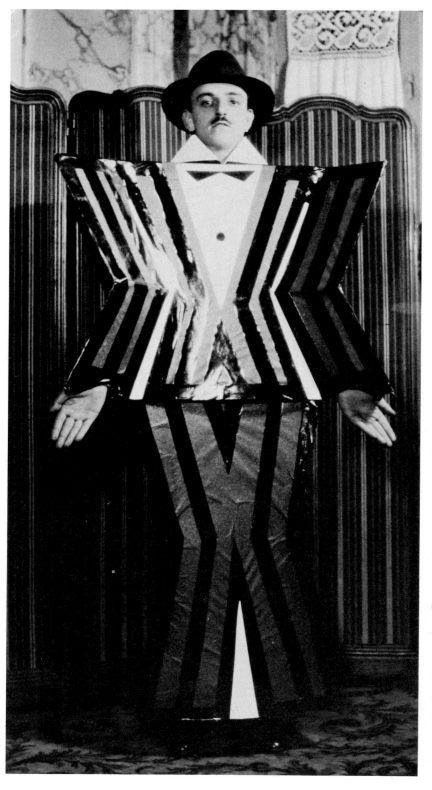

146

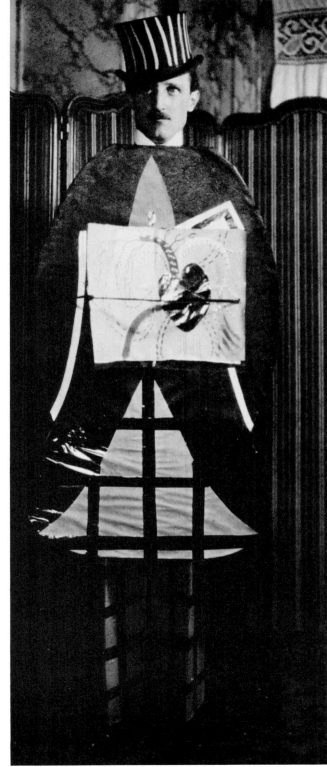

148

Poem written by Vladimir Mayakovsky on a door painted by Delaunay, 1926.

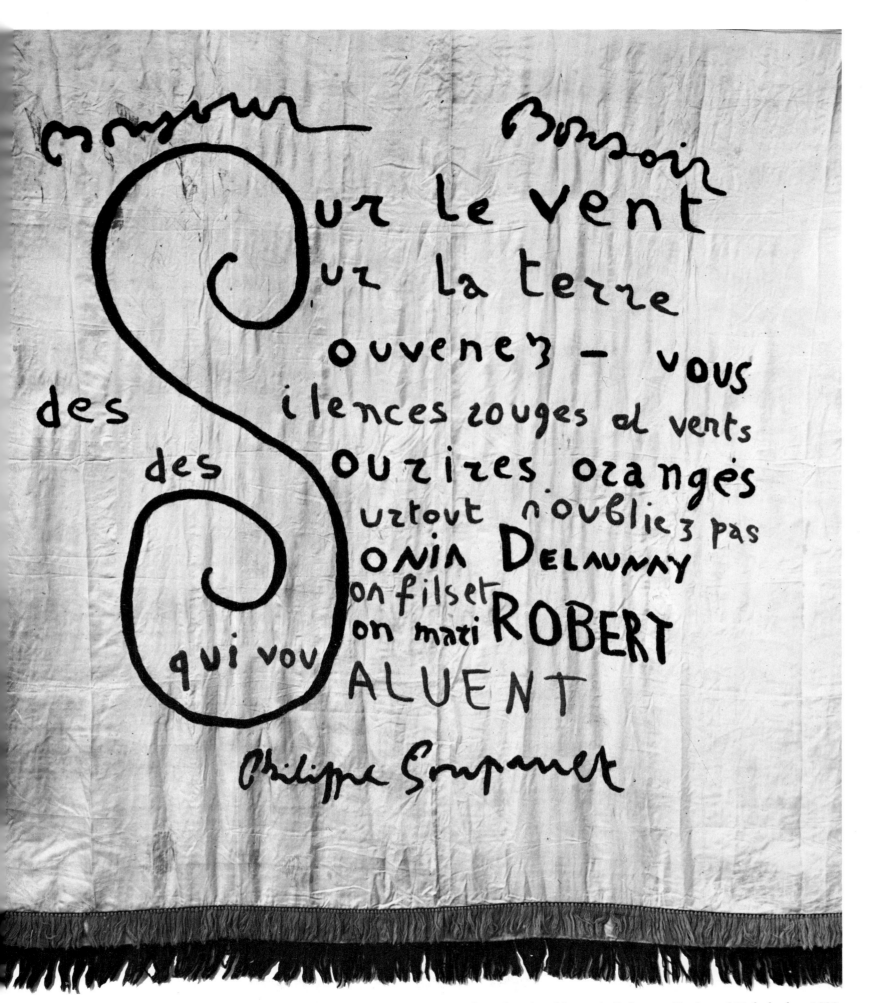

Curtain-poem by Philippe Soupault, embroidered by Sonia Delaunay, Boulevard Malesherbes, 1922.

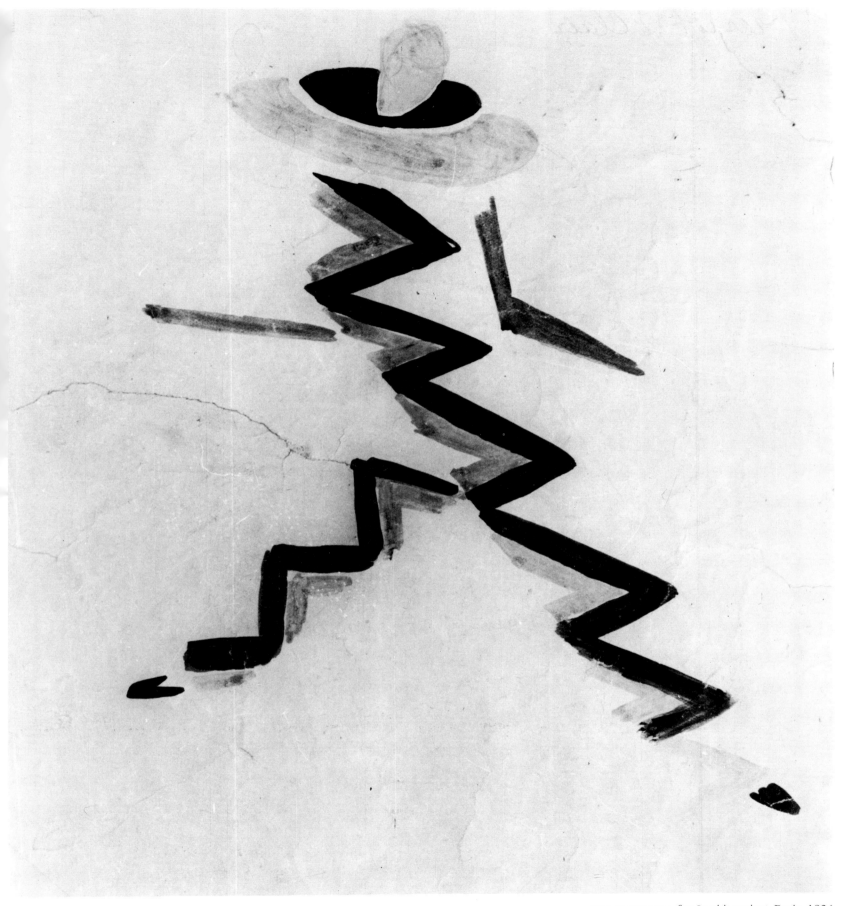

Dance costume for *Le p'tit parigot*. Paris, 1926.
Watercolour on paper; 22.5 × 19 cm.
Costume design for the film *Le p'tit parigot*, directed by R. Le Somptier.

Poem Dress. Paris, 1922; Watercolour. 35.7 × 30 cm; no. 686.

151

Fashion

As early as 1911, Sonia Delaunay had already had the idea of making a silk patchwork blanket for her new-born son, thereby transposing into artistic terms a Russian peasant custom. Thereafter the Delaunay's flat in the Rue des Grands-Augustins took on a new look. Originally it had been decorated in a typical bourgeois style with wallpaper and Empire and Louis-Philippe furniture, which went well with the paintings of the Douanier Rousseau which they had acquired after his death. Nevertheless things slowly began to change. First Sonia lined the walls with white calico, then she made patchwork cushions and lampshades to decorate the rooms. These were the first steps that Sonia Delaunay took towards something which was to become a total revolution, visually as well as in the art of living.

At about the same time, she set about illustrating the covers and fly-leaves of Cendrars' poem *Pâques* with original collages which owed nothing to Cubism. Her husband's tailor had given her multi-coloured samples of materials with which she decided to compose a dress inspired from her painting. This first 'simultaneous' dress corresponded exactly to their aesthetic preoccupations of that period, and it was this very same one that Blaise Cendrars described in 1914: *Sur la robe elle a un corps* (On her dress she wears a body). On this occasion, Guillaume Apollinaire wrote in the 1 January 1914 number of the *Mercure de France*: 'Monsieur and Madame Robert Delaunay have undertaken to reform costume. It is imperative to go to the Bullier and see what they are doing.

'The innovations in the way of clothing brought about by simultaneous Orphism are not to be disregarded. These could have inspired a curious chapter in Carlyle's *Sartor Resartus*. The

Delaunays are innovators. But in so far as they neither care for outworn fashions, nor seek to depart from the styles of their own times, their innovation lies in their desire to influence fashion through new textures and a great diversity of colours.

'Take for example one of M. Robert Delaunay's costumes: purple jacket, beige waistcoat, dusky black trousers. Or this one: red coat with a blue collar, red socks, black and yellow shoes, green jacket, sky-blue waistcoat and, at last, a tiny red tie.

'To complete the picture, here is one of Mme Delaunay's simultaneous dresses: a purple costume with a long purple and green belt, underneath a blouse which is divided into areas of different colours, bright, gentle or faded, intermingled with shades of salmon-pink, yellowy-orange, powder-blue and scarlet. It is made up of juxtaposed fabrics of varying kinds such as taffeta, organdie, flannelette and pou-de-soie.

'Such diversity has not passed unnoticed. She has combined fantasy with elegance.

'And if you do happen to go to the Bullier, and if you do not manage to catch a glimpse of them straight away, know that these innovators have their place next to the orchestra. From this vantage point, they can contemplate, without the least scorn, the monotonous costumes of the dancers.'

In 1922, a firm of Lyon silk manufacturers commissioned fifty designs for materials from Sonia Delaunay. After a brief moment of hesitation, she realized that this was a marvellous opportunity for her to further the study of colour which she had already undertaken in her painting. This was how geometrical and abstract patterns were introduced into printed textiles from 1923 onwards. As Robert Delaunay points out:

153

'Up till then, materials were largely printed replicas of designs which the Ballets Russes had brought back into fashion before the war. The vogue of Orientalism had also become widespread. The materials in fashion displayed large colourful flowers on brightly coloured backgrounds, or else tangles of different types of flowers, like poppies, cornflowers and rose garlands, printed in gold on a black background. Indeed, fashion had been overrun by all the flowers of creation printed in lavish colours. The world of fabric design was to be profoundly altered by Sonia Delaunay's work.'

Scarves, ballet costumes, embroidered waistcoats (made to order for Jacques Doucet and René Crevel) and embroidered coats succeeded each other and were sold all over the world. They were almost all based on collage. Most of her work in this line was shown to the public in 1923, in the fashion booth she set up at the Bal Bullier; everything in the booth, from floor to ceiling, including the costumes worn by the models, was a collage.

Economic and social evolution also had its influence on dress. The growing numbers of working women, the extension of their civil rights, their access to jobs previously reserved for men, all encouraged them to adapt their way of dressing to the new requirements of daily life. What had only been a necessity of wartime slowly became a new way of life. Fashion needed to be practical for a woman who had more freedom than before, who now exercised a profession, played a sport and danced. The waist-line and bust were neglected and the skirt shortened; she cut her hair and wore pyjamas. These were the women men found on their

return from the war, companions with neat, young silhouettes and a masculine gait. This was indeed a surprise, but then it had a new appeal, that of the tomboy.

Haute couture did not accept this change with immediate enthusiasm, and soon certain fashion houses lost their influence. Establishments such as Doucet, Dœuillet and Drecoll closed down, and so did Paul Poiret — his famous fashion barges for the 1925 exhibition were his swan-song — but new establishments opened up. Quite in keeping with the times, women now dominated the scene and renewed the prestige of Parisian elegance. Among those who were in the limelight for the next twenty years were Madame Gerver, Madame Paquin, Jeanne Lanvin, Madeleine Vonnet, Chanel — and of course Sonia Delaunay.

Another innovation of this era, was that sportswear now entered the fashion scene, for motoring, tennis, golf, winter sports, and the beach. Originality was the keynote, whether it was in knitwear, bathing-costumes or travelling-clothes — that is to say, gracefulness and inventiveness were sought in clothes which, until then, had been merely serviceable. On the whole there was less ornamentation on clothes; but technical advances in materials made up for this loss. Alongside the then popular dull or shimmering satins, there were also new fabrics, which had just appeared on the market: georgette, muslin embroidered with metal, Scottish wool, and so on.

Black and white were still in favour, as well as the pre-war taste for having evening dresses, scarves and shawls in rich fabrics and violent colours. Paul Poiret continued to use the bright, firm colours that Serge de Diaghilev's Ballets Russes had brought into fashion fifteen years earlier. Artists like Paul Iribe and Raoul Dufy remained under his influence.

'Short, flat, geometrical and quadrangular, feminine wear is fixed along the outline of the parallelogram; and 1925 shall not see the come-back of soft curves, arrogant breasts and enticing hips', wrote Colette in *Vogue.*

The form reduced to its principal lines makes one shape out of the costume, so that in certain paintings of Braque and Picasso, bewildered onlookers were unable to distinguish where the artist intended to place the bust or the legs.

But Sonia Delaunay's perspectives were quite different; she did not make use of violent colours gratuitously, as Poiret recommended; she did not compose Cubist or Futurist costumes either. With a great deal of good sense, she created dresses and coats which betrayed neither the artist nor the woman in her. Her printed materials were a tremendous success, and were exported in bulk to foreign countries. Her 1925 album was packed with ideas and Blaise Cendrars was right when he wrote to her on 10 November 1925:

'Dear Madame,

'In Paris for a few days, I was today given the album you kindly sent to me, for which very many thanks. . . . If, alas, my poem is still up-to-date, I am above all, sorry that one doesn't see more of your dresses around town. Black has become too much of a habit with these ladies, as if they were Romantic poets! Poverty and good taste are not yet dressed in the bright colours of a parasol, but always seem to go in pairs like the horses of a hearse. The whole world seems to be in mourning, and that's too bad. Cordially yours.'

In the lecture she once gave at the Sorbonne, Sonia Delaunay pointed out that though she had sought to adapt fashion to the practical requirements of life, the surface of a piece of material could still offer scope for untold fantasy and imagination.

The importance of the International Exhibition of Decorative Arts, held in Paris in 1925, is hard to overestimate. Among other things, it provided the manufacturers of artistic and luxury goods with their first great opportunity to exhibit since the war. The exhibition was inaugurated on 18 July 1925. The preparations not being quite ready for the inauguration, it was nicknamed with untranslatable facetiousness 'L'Exposition des Arts décors hâtifs'.

Armand Lanoux wrote:

'President Doumergue makes his official tour of the exhibition. Plump and good-natured, he leads his herd of top-hatted official visitors to the Pavilion of Elegance. Amid the disturbing array of Siegel's streamlined mannequins, four couturières hold the floor, Callot, Jenny, Lanvin and Worth, not counting the Sonia Delaunay and Jacques Heim boutique. The Soviet pavilion faces the German one. . . .The Tour de Paris stands erect and the esplanade of the Invalides resounds with the noise of loud-speakers.

'President Doumergue seems a little bewildered, surrounded as he is by Negro music, the diamond-merchants' pavilion, sculpture in reinforced concrete by Mallet-Stevens, department stores and their art workshops, Pomona's upholstery, Primavera gone Negro, the savoir-faire of the Galeries Lafayette, the ideal flat of 'Lewis and Irene' by Gomina, Captain Paul Poiret on his barges *Amour, Delice* and *Orgue*. And the presidential visitor keeps on walking, wending his way among Dunand lacquers, Rodier textiles, Cartier jewels, Bagues chandeliers, Hermes leathers. 157

'The journalists have unanimously proclaimed Sonia Delaunay's boutique on the Pont Alexandre III as outstanding. There we can feast our eyes on her "simultaneous" materials and fabulous embroidery, executed as always with great care for harmony of colour. These magnificent coats in graduated tints, delicate as morning mists or reflections of autumnal splendours, must have been made for regal shoulders. Sonia Delaunay also works in furs with unsurpassed virtuosity, and she knows how to play off neutral shades of skins against one another. She combines fur with embroidery, metal with wool or silk — but the metals she uses are always dull in colour, thus creating a certain rich, discreet elegance.'

'These "simultaneous" fabrics are intended', wrote Delteil, 'to suggest movement, one of a whole system of interlocking movements — comparable to a dynamic conception of the Universe.'

Sonia Delaunay's *Album 1925* had recently been published, and was greeted thus in the periodical *Les Nouvelles littéraires* by Florent Fels:

'Turning over the pages of this album, I know I shall rediscover the whole gamut of brilliant singing colours imagined by one of today's most extraordinary creators. I use the word "creator" intentionally, for Sonia Delaunay has rejuvenated fashion and the decorative arts — in the same way as Alexandre Benois and Bakst revolutionized theatre design, and as later the Ballets Russes revolutionized fashion.'

This album set the seal on Sonia Delaunay's discoveries; but soon her ideas were plundered by her rivals.

Poets and painters unanimously declared that the relationships created by Sonia Delaunay partook of poetry — a poetry not exempt from usefulness, and achieved through the simplest of means, a few colours, geometrical forms, dashes of strong colour juxtaposed in a brilliant fashion, and the whole coordinated in delightful harmony. These models of dresses, of materials, of carpets, were filled with a wealth of imagination so that one felt as though one had assisted at some magnificent ceremony.

Of course, as Robert Delaunay reminds us, 'simultaneous materials originated in the most modern trends in painting which had evolved around 1912 and which, since then, have been developed in Paris. It was in her painting that Sonia Delaunay found the basic elements which enabled her to create her designs for her materials.'

160

Sports suit. Paris, 1923. Watercolour on paper. 43 × 29 cm; no. 865.

161

Dance costume. Paris, 1923. Watercolour on paper. 36 × 28 cm; no. 674.

Costumes for *Le Cœur à gaz* by Tristan Tzara. Paris, 1923.
Left: Tzara. Watercolour on paper. 39 × 29 cm; no. 679.
Right: René Crevel. Watercolour on paper. 43 × 29 cm; no. 277.

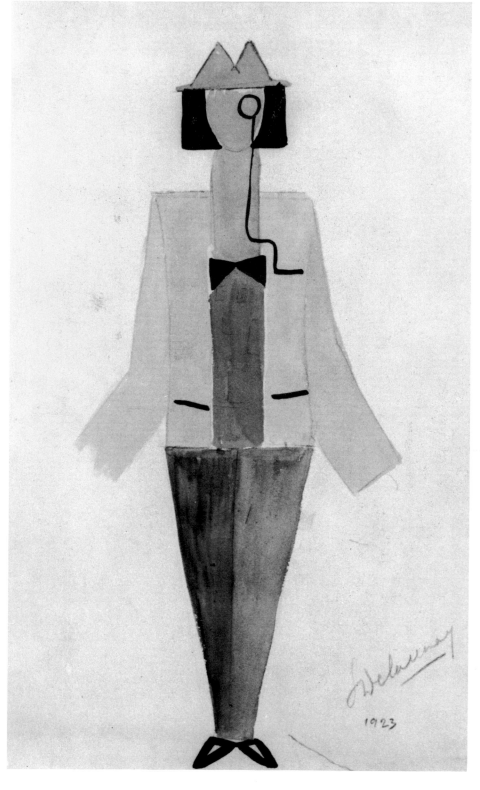

Costume for the Rio carnival.
Paris, 1923. 36 × 25 cm; no. 215.

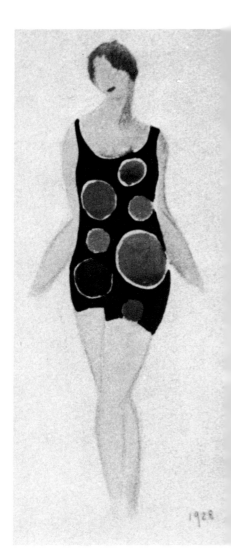

Three sketches for bathing costumes, 1928.

Black and white bathing costume made and worn by Sonia Delaunay at Carnac in 1928, holidaying with Arp, Tzara, Sophie Taeuber and Huidobro.

THE COMING FASHION

To Mme Sonia Delaunay

(ON STAGE IS A RECITER IN FULL EVENING DRESS)

The coming fashion is profound and mysterious, to speak of it gives
*   rhythm to my tongue and I feel myself caught up in its flow.*
It comes like a sentient being, and henceforth, as has been said,
*   on her dress woman wears a body.*
All is mystery in silk
In wool and in cotton
The art of cutting out a dress
Is part miracle, part measure; in the beginning of fashion there
*   is God.*
No, no, no, it is not true that God created woman naked,
But he gave her a dress from the very beginning, a silk dress,
Open to paradise,
Which had the shape of birds and the colour of angels.
It was after she sinned that God took away her dress.
No, nakedness, wearisome nakedness, is not *the most glorious*
*   costume,*
But rather
A scrap of cloth against the skin;
For cloth is ideal and divine,
Cloth which is elusive as swallows,
Cloth which has a thousand names and origins,
From that which is born at a ewe's udder,
And that which a paradisal worm creates in a sunny mood,
To those which nest on equatorial trees,
To those which have sprung from the little flowers of the fields,
All cloths,
Meltingly soft like eyes in tears,
Sombre, and bad for those with weak hearts,
Flimsy, and revealing young delicate chests,
Falling in folds around big businessmen,
Heavy stuffs, heavier than death itself,
and others lighter than life,
Those which are at home in the unfathomed,
And those whose charm is a tissue of fraud and error
Around her, here are the products of nature, lizards and fruits,
Plants, gems, scales and quails.

Black, brown and beige costume, 1924;
Brown, black and yellow check costume, 1923;
Bœuf sur le toit coat, black, blue and red, 1922;
Brown, beige and black check coat, 1926;
Black and grey jacket over a black dress;
Tennis costume, 1925, grey with black trimmings and
a black, red and blue blouse.

For my desire is to use all materials,
Fur and horsehair, which are eloquent voices,
Leather which has something royal about it,
Parchment, symbol of intelligence, joy of the mind,
Glass, glass in bloom,
Paper which is like clouds and tea-roses,
and possibly slate and possibly wood.
And who knows? metals, which are full of the Earth's secrets,
Red metal, green metal, and that which has no definite colour.
I love colours that merge, composite, elusive,
Those which neither great minds nor hoary chemists can name
Those which are joy, optimism and plenitude,
Those which are akin to scarabs and little illustrious insects,
Those which are redolent of flesh and nature's outcome,
Those which are slightly phenomenal and respectfully deceive the
    eye,
I love secret colours,
Naked colours,
Those which are a movement, an orb and a revolution.

       All lines lead to the heart.

       The sleeves are the wings of the heart.

       The socks the colour of the heart.

       The boots strike up the rhythm of the heart.

       The trousers climb the heart.

       The waistcoat is the knave of the heart.

       The necktie is the knot of the heart.

       The buttonhole is the flower of the heart.

       All lines lead to the heart,

       All lines lead to the heart!

Round speed maddens our tissues and our legs.
Blood gallops in our veins to the rhythm of the Universe.
Nothing will ever stop our pulses or the turning earth.
A dress is no longer a little, flat, closed thing,
But begins in the open sky and mingles with the courses of the stars,
So that she who wears it carries the world on her back.
The Universe is at Woman's beck and call.
Woman is the centre of everything.
Around her, here are the products of nature, lizards and fruits,
Plants, gems, scales and quails.

Black, blue and grey coat, 1925.

For it is our desire to use all materials,
Fur and horsehair, which are eloquent voices,
Leather which has something royal about it,
Parchment, symbol of intelligence, joy of the mind,
Glass, glass in bloom,
Paper which is like clouds and tea-roses,
and possibly slate and possibly wood,
And who knows? metals, which are full of the Earth's secrets,
Red metal, green metal, and that which has no definite colour.
For we love colours that merge, composite, elusive,
Those which neither great minds nor hoary chemists can name,
Those which are joy, optimism and plenitude,
Those which are akin to scarabs and little colourless insects,
Those which are redolent of flesh and the matter of nature,
Those which are slightly phenomenal and respectfully mysterious,
We love secret colours,
Naked colours,
Those which are a movement, an orb and a revolution.
Those whose wefts take wing, whose warps dance like atoms
A need for speed maddens our tissues, our hearts and our legs.
Blood gallops in our veins to the rhythm of the Universe.
Nothing will ever stop our pulses or the turning earth.
Our feet slip endlessly on the highwire of celestial parabolas
A dress is no longer a little, flat, closed thing
But begins in the open sky and mingles with the courses of the stars.
So that she who wears it carries the world on her back
All in us is vibration, attraction and gravitation
Here are our hats dancing and our coats around us
Immobility is dead, and this is the reign of movement
Movement which is born at the heels and spreads through every
        fibre,
The circular coloured movement which is at the centre of every-
        thing, which is everything,
Essential rhythm
The dance
'The dance began a moment ago
For a little it swells, engulfs
Men and fabrics, and drowns the voice.'

JOSEPH DELTEIL

POEM FOR A DRESS
BY MADAME SONIA DELAUNAY

*The angel has slipped his hand
into the basket, the eye of the fruit.
He arrests the wheels of the motor cars
and the human heart's dizzy gyroscope.*

TRISTAN TZARA

Black and ochre coat, 1923.

Sketches for a fancy-dress ball: spinning top; coat for the top. Paris, 1923.

'Cabman coat' in brown,
beige and black, 1923-1924.

Costume with blue, green red and black
jacket over red and black skirt, 1924;
Black and white dress, 1924;
Grey, black and white dress, 1924-25;
Black, green and grey dress, 1925.

Lady in blue, 1924; Black, white and red dress, 1922; Design for black, grey and blue dress, 1923.

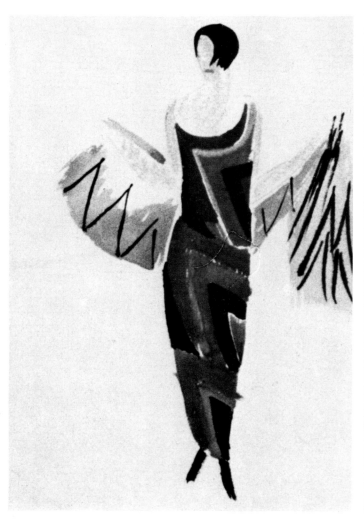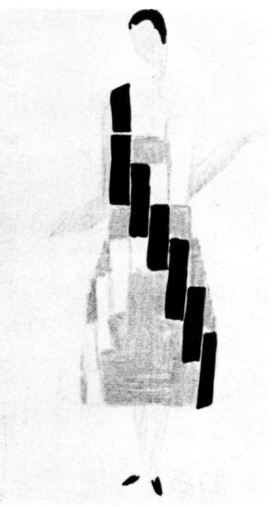

EVENING DRESS BY MADAME SONIA DELAUNAY

Let us forget the birds
the stars in the night
make signs for all eternity
and the cold descends
without a sound.
Let us forget the stars
the snow in the sky
flies gently
all our lives
let us forget the birds, the snow and the stars.

PHILIPPE SOUPAULT

Black, green and blue coat, 1923; Beige and brown coat, 1924; Black, grey and red coat, 1924.

1922

Black, grey and blue evening dress,
1922;
Black, red and green dress, 1926;
Grey, black and ochre dress and
matching hat, 1925;
'Monastic' dress, 1922.

POEM FOR THE DRESS OF THE FUTURE

To Madame Sonia Delaunay

In the beginning was a dress, a silken dress,
Open to Paradise,
Which had the shape of birds and the colour of angels.

> *All is mystery in silk,*
> *In wool and in cotton;*
> *The art of cutting out a dress*
> *Is part miracle, part measure.*

Of cloth I sing
Cloth which has a thousand names and origins,
From that which is born at a ewe's udder,
And that which a paradisal worm creates in a sunny mood,
To those which nest on equatorial trees;
To those which have sprung from the little flowers of the fields,
All cloths
Meltingly soft like eyes in tears,
Coarse, and bad for those with weak hearts,
Thick-grained, and bestowing square-edged caresses,
Flimsy, and revealing young delicate chests,
And those which fall in folds round big businessmen,
Heavy stuffs, heavier than death itself,
And others lighter than life,
Those which are at home in the unfathomed,
and those whose charm is a tissue of fraud and error,
And those which bite, and those which bleed,
And even those whose beauty is made up of monstrous treasures . . .
What a fabulous object woman will be!
A quintessence of the Universe!
She will borrow her line from the natural elements,
From all that flows and flies, from rivers and from snakes.
She dresses in animal skins, in rainbows and leaves from trees.
She usurps the tint of the forests and of evening, the uncertain, total tint.
She seizes with a swift movement all that passes, all that flees,
She is at the centre of Matter and Matter is her child
And those which bite and those which bleed,
And even those whose beauty is mingled with monstrous treasures . . .
And these same men, see them clad in the triangular mode.
The one who is no doubt a businessman and perhaps a man of feeling,
He has no awareness of wearing a miracle on his torso;

Well, he is a consequence of the choicest astronomical theories;

And this other whose pince-nez are a bicycle rolling across his pupils,

And this one has on his soft hat

showered torrents of stick;

And that one, who has abandoned the straight line and the short linear
    conception,

And the paltry rules of silhouette single material and flat colour,

To leap at last into the wide virgin expanses,

The regions of fashion round

Like the world

Yes, all of us poets, bankers, sportsmen and pursuers of speed,

We have continued on our clothes the parabolas of the planets,

All the lines of the Universe end at our Centre.

All lines lead to the heart.

The arabesque of our hats, along the neck, continues to the heart,

The sleeves are the wings of the heart

The socks the colour of the heart

The boots have their centre of gravity right in the heart

The trousers climb the heart

The waistcoat is the knave of the heart

The necktie is the knot of the heart

The buttonhole is the flower of the heart

All lines lead to the heart (Twice; the echo repeats)

All lines lead to the heart (and the women enter)

Oh! What a fabulous thing woman will become!

A quintessence of the Universe!

She will borrow her line from the natural elements,

From all that flows and flies, from a river, from a snake.

She will dress in animal skins, in rainbows and leaves from trees.

She usurps the tint of the forests and of the evening, the uncertain,
    composite tint

She seizes with a swift movement all that passes, all that flees.

Immobility is dead and this is the reign of movement

Movement is born at the heels to spread among the stars,

The circular coloured movement which is at the centre of everything,
    which is everything.

And look, a dress is a dance.

178   JOSEPH DELTEIL

each coat in black, red and white printed material, 1925;
vening dress in black tulle, embroidered with
lk strands forming coloured discs, 1926.
usée Nissim de Camondo, Paris.

Beige and grey dress, 1926;
Hand-embroidered coat in
graduated shades of grey, 1925;
Plain coat with a geometrical
border, 1924;
Printed raincoat, 1926.

Hand-embroidered coat,
worn by Nancy Cunard, 1925.

Robert and Sonia Delaunay posing in front of his painting *Propeller*, 1923.

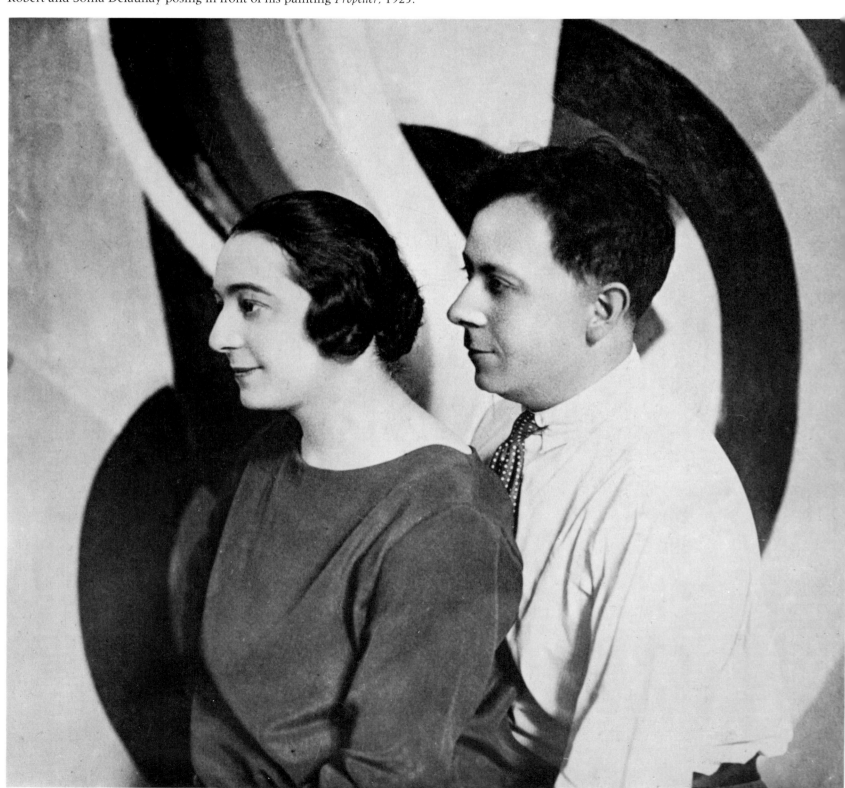

Sonia Delaunay and two friends draped in her materials, Rue des Grands-Augustins, 1924.
On the left, Robert Delaunay's *Propeller,* and on the right, his *Homage to Blériot.*

Costume for the Rio carnival, 1928,
and sketch for Apache dance, 1928.

Dance costume. Paris, 1923. Watercolour on paper. 29 × 23 cm; no. 672.

185

Sonia Delaunay in Madrid, 1918. Raffia hat, sunshade and sleeveless sweater.

Sonia Delaunay in her studio, Boulevard Malesherbes, 1924.

187

188 Spiral, red and pink costume for the 1928 Rio carnival.

Black, grey and white dress for *Le p'tit parigot*, film by Le Somptier, 1926.

Star. Blue and yellow printed material, 1926.

Sonia Delaunay

1925

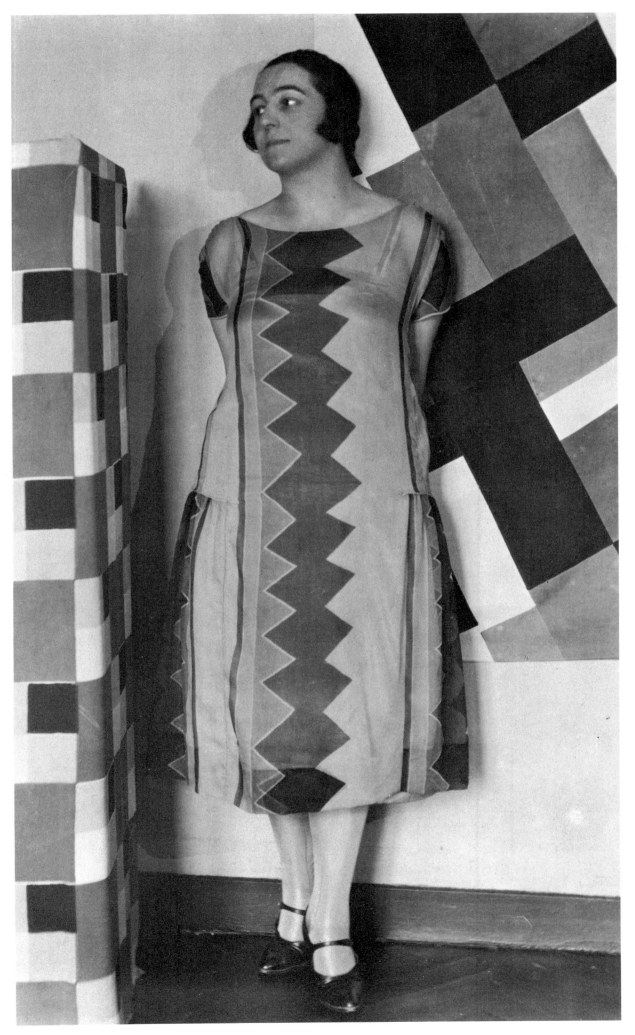

Costume designs for the
Decorative Arts Exhibition, 1925.
Indian ink. 27 × 20 cm.

Sonia Delaunay wearing
one of her dresses, 1925.

191

192   Two projects for ballet stage sets, 1928-1929. Gouache on paper. 21.5 × 27 cm.

194   Material with wavy design, exhibited on a model by Siegel
made of facetted mirrors. Pavillon de Marsan, 1930.

Embroidered coat for Gloria Swanson, 1923.

onia Delaunay draped in one of her first shawls, Boulevard Malesherbes, 1925.

Printed textile, 1926.

ecorative Arts Exhibition, Paris 1925.
onia Delaunay and Jacques Heim's Boutique
imultanée, on the Pont Alexandre III.

Black and white scarf, approximately
six feet long, 1922.

Material with striped squares, 1924.

Material with red, blue and black stripes on white, 1923.

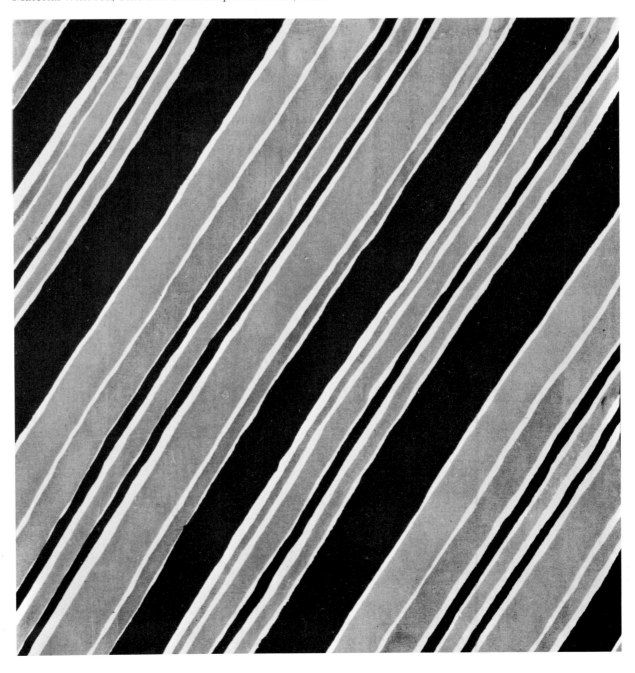

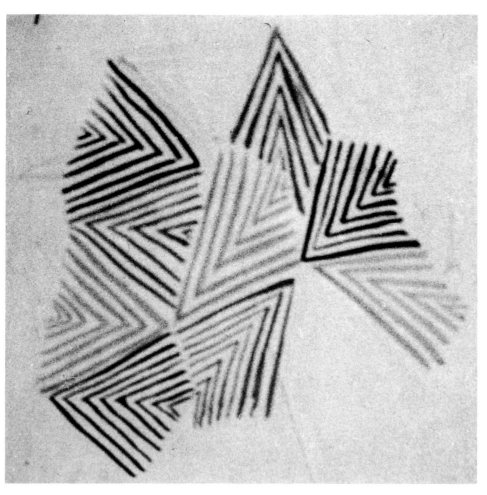

202

Drawing in indian ink, 1922;
Sketch for red, green and blue material
on black background, 1924.

Textile design, 1925.

ess design, 1922. Watercolour on paper. No. 403.

Decorative Arts Exhibition, Paris 1925. The Boutique Simultanée, on the Pont Alexandre III.

Decorative Arts Exhibition, Paris, 1925. Mannequins wearing embroidered coats, a dress and pyjamas designed by Sonia Delaunay; sculpture in reinforced concrete by Mallet-Stevens; interior by Pierre Chareau.

Textile design with black background, 1930. Gouach

Textile design, 1930; Indian ink.

Textile designs, 1929:
typographical experiments and 'Venus'.

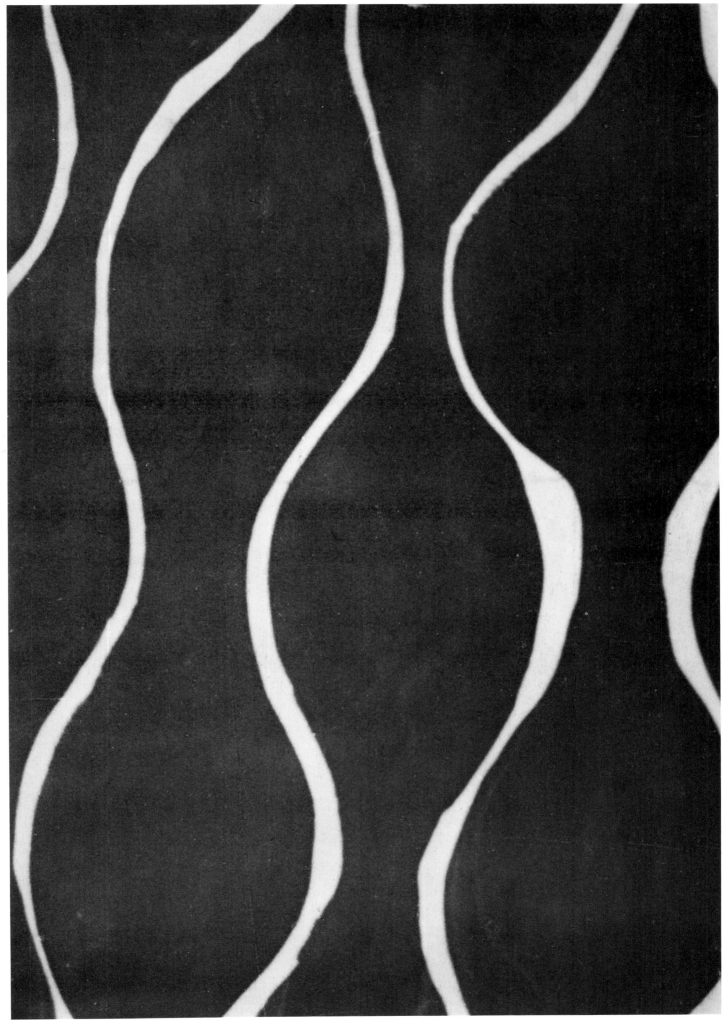

onia Delaunay in her studio, Boulevard Malesherbes, 1924.
Photograph by Geneviève Krull.

Three models, wearing clothes designed by Sonia Delaunay, in front of the Delaunays' Talbot in 1928.

Heim's models wearing clothes designed by Sonia Delaunay, posing in front of a journalist's 5-CV Citroën, which was painted in imitation of one of Sonia Delaunay's textile designs.

Textile design,
for silk print, 1923.
Gouache. No. 6.

217

Textile designs, 1926 : 'Labyrinth' and 'Chanel'.

Textile design inspired by African art, 1924.

Textile design for silk print, 1926: 'Spiral'.

Black, white and brown carpet, 1926.

Sonia Delaunay, 1930.
Photograph by Florence Henri.

The Delaunays' sitting-room, Boulevard Malesherbes, 1925.
The walls are hung with printed linen in different shades of
beige, the armchairs are upholstered with hand-embroidered
materials. All, including the carpet, were designed by the artist.

Cabinet in maple veneer, designed by Sonia Delaunay, 1924.

Black and white printed materials, 1925-1926.

228

Project for the
dining-room of the
Boulevard Malesherbes
flat, 1924.

Study of optical effects. Textile design, 1933. 18 × 16.5 cm; no. 1440. An anticipation of Op art.

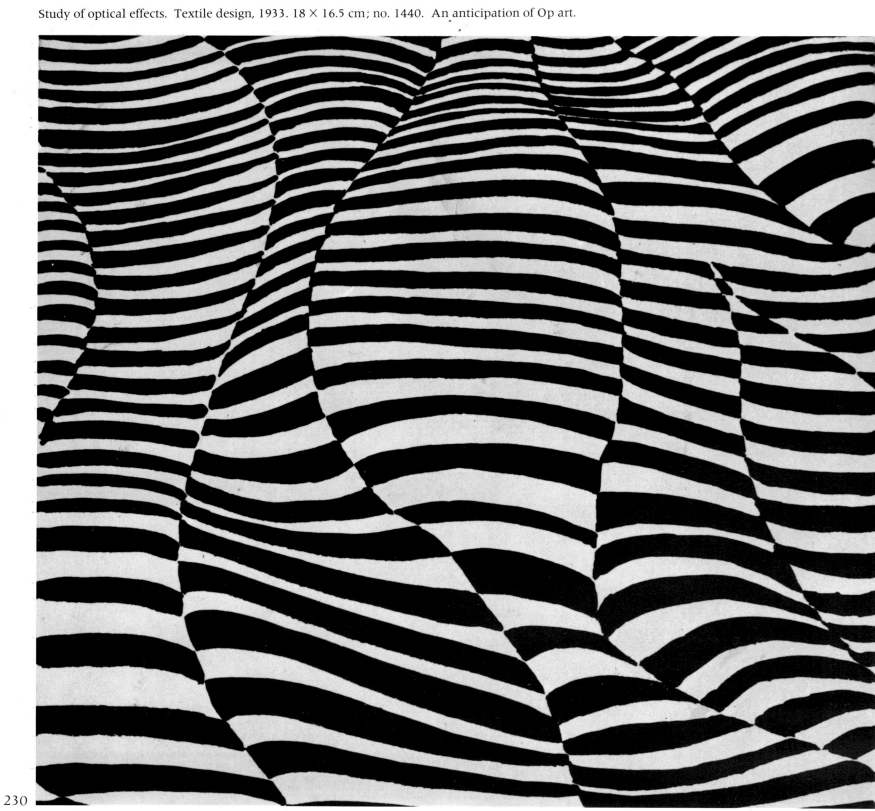

The 1937 Exhibition

Sonia Delaunay working in the Levallois garage-workshop on her murals for the 1937 International Exhibition.

The 1937 Exhibition

On 24 May, the 1937 International Exhibition was inaugurated. The eagle grasping the swastika of the Third Reich in its claws arrogantly confronted the hammer and sickle. These were stirring times, and no one really knew what the future would bring. Spain was in the midst of Civil War, the German Führer ruthlessly pursued his rise to power and the delicate political equilibrium of Europe was slowly disintegrating. Nonetheless political events did not prevent the Delaunays from continuing their work. Without really ignoring them, they seemed unperturbed by the darkening clouds of political unrest and, certain that their creations would last, they carried on working.

One reads in a newspaper of that year, 'The organizers of the 1937 Exhibition have decided to welcome all schools of painting. One cannot but admire the wisdom with which the decors envisaged have been shared out; in fact, one is filled with admiration to think that they have achieved a perfect formula: speed = abstract art.'

The decoration of the Railways and Aeronautics pavilions had been commissioned from a group of young artists, who had all been influenced from an early age by the effects of Cubism. The leading painter was Robert Delaunay. The story goes that when Raoul Dautry, then Minister of Transport and Communications, had seen Robert Delaunay's preliminary sketches for the Railways pavilion (the old, disused Gare des Invalides had been selected to house the pavilion), and after having carefully studied the series of frenzied circles, endlessly reflected squares and fleeting rays of colour, said simply: 'This is altogether admirable. I'm going to have our latest types of signals sent to you — you might find them useful.'

Delaunay and his team took over a large garage near the Porte de Champerret as a workshop. Cubicles like monastic cells were hurriedly fitted out into rooms for each member of the team, and everyone set to work on the hundreds of square metres to be painted. 'This seminary of pure colour had to be seen to be believed,' one of the participants tells us. 'Life was marvellous and spirits were high. We all had the faith of the medieval illuminators and painted with the frenzy of decorators preparing stage sets. We were modest, for we were only copying models which had already been approved, but undoubtedly we put in our best to recreate them, decomposing them according to the strictest geometrical methods, all the while careful not to betray their inspiration.'

In the *Petit Parisien* of 30 May 1937, a journalist, Jean Maréchal, describes the atmosphere in which Sonia and Robert Delaunay worked on the project: 'I cannot explain why I had imagined these workshops of abstract art as mysterious laboratories where reigned a half-light favourable to the creation of obscure and somewhat incomprehensible works. Instead of an alchemist's den, I discovered, in an immense garage and amid makeshift arrangements, an outburst of enthusiasm, of light, of springtime. . . . A group of young artists — men and women together — were feverishly working to complete the murals intended for the Railways and Aeronautics pavilions. Here, dressed in bright yellow trousers and light brown sweater, Robert Delaunay was busy putting the finishing touches to a folded canvas ready to be sent to the Exhibition — I could only appreciate the freshness and harmony of the tones from the model. . . . There, Sonia Delaunay was completing another canvas for the

234

Railways pavilion — a composition displaying numerous stylized, yet both picturesque and evocative characters.'

Maréchal is no doubt referring here to the composition entitled *Journeys Far Away*, for which Sonia Delaunay was awarded a gold medal. Though the lightly sketched preliminary gouache brings out an underlying structure of concatenated circular forms, the final work is figurative, the circular forms becoming transposed into stylized people or parasols. He goes on:

'It is really quite exceptional to come across such a homogeneous team where each one has sacrificed his own individuality to a single aesthetic inspiration, and gives the best of himself, of his ardour and of his talent to a common work. And when the Delaunays set down their paint-brushes for an instant, it is not to devote themselves to the occult practices of abstract art. as I had secretly hoped, but to celebrate the joy they find in working together, the sincere fellowship which unites them. This, in their view, is "tomorrow's formula", something quite new in social as well as artistic terms, an experiment with world-wide implications, and one which must succeed. They speak with smiling conviction.

'One cannot but share their opinion when one looks upon this fascinating blossoming of forms and colours, and when one sees with what energy these young people are imparting dynamism and cheerfulness to their work. When I leave, and the garage doors close upon this dazzling wonderland of singing colours, I take away the unforgettable impression of a team of young people, perhaps the first who have managed to show us what can be achieved artistically when unstinted effort is united with a freely-accepted discipline.'

Constructed entirely out of metal, the Aeronautical Pavilion stood on the corner of the Esplanade des Invalides and the Quai d'Orsay. The pavilion was an immense 85 foot-high windowed hall, roofed with a single 115 foot span. In the original plans conceived by Delaunay, it was to be entirely covered in Rhodoïd, a thermoplastic material that was to be used here for the first time in building. A narrow gangway of the same material, suspended from the middle of the hall, allowed people to move around the planes which were exhibited.

Another reporter wrote, 'This transparent palace allows us to see its multi-coloured intestines. From close up, these become light-blue and pink catwalks which rise in the wake of invisible aeroplanes, and criss-cross on high, among the impressive machines. Down below, the walls of the hall are covered with magnificent murals designed by Sonia Delaunay, Jacques Villon, Crotti and Gleizes.'

The abstract character of their art symbolized a science which was rapidly overtaking both man and nature, yet, in its very dynamism, their work expressed a faith in progress which went beyond the oppression of man by machines. The immense panels painted by Robert and Sonia Delaunay were a perfect background for an aerodynamic display. Both the Delaunays were interested in aviation; in 1914 Robert Delaunay had painted his famous *Homage to Blériot,* and years later they had both been to Le Bourget airport to see Lindbergh land.

An essentially dynamic and triumphant pictorial symphony had been composed from iridescent circles, the prisms and diagonal lines, and multi-coloured segments. It was a world

where mathematical precision was combined with quivering

speed, where everything whistled, crackled, grated, exploded and whirled. The rigorous compositional discipline underlying such tumultuousness corresponded perfectly to the new world of technology, the track diagrams, the engineers' icy blueprints, the cross-sections of locomotives displaying their constellation of twinkling dials, and the discs and semaphore signals. One might think of this merely as an 'abstract image' — but does not this concept admirably translate the mysteries of industrialized science? There are, however, other more precise, more figurative images which emerge out of the multi-coloured web, seeming somehow to be part of them; as though they were the evocation of mechanical rhythms pertaining to the domain of pure sensation.

'Delaunay's work presents us with a synthesis of Paris', wrote Louis Cheronnet. 'We behold a tremendous effulgence of luminous rays pouring forth from the gigantic pylon of the Eiffel Tower. Paris, turned into a glorious Central Station! Sonia Delaunay for her part, leads us into a wondrous land, among the magical spheres of optical illusion and invisible electrical currents. The idea of the infinitely small and the infinitely big makes us quite dizzy. We are surrounded by a magical play of light diffractions and electrical interferences, of fissions and fusions. A realm of illusion where time can only be a dream. Walking through the Aeronautical Pavilion we finally arrive in a vast hall which resembles the cockpit of an over-sized aeroplane ready to soar up into space. Within the convex, luminous cockpit one observes several planes which seem to float among the spirals of a celestial yet half real staircase. How could one better express the exaltation of one of Man's latest conquests?' 237

Sonia Delaunay and her assistants working on her murals for the 1937 International Exhibition.

The 1937 International Exhibition. Mural: *Journeys Far Away* in the Railways Pavilion.

The 1937 International Exhibition: work on the murals
for the Aeronautical Pavilion and the Railways Pavilion.

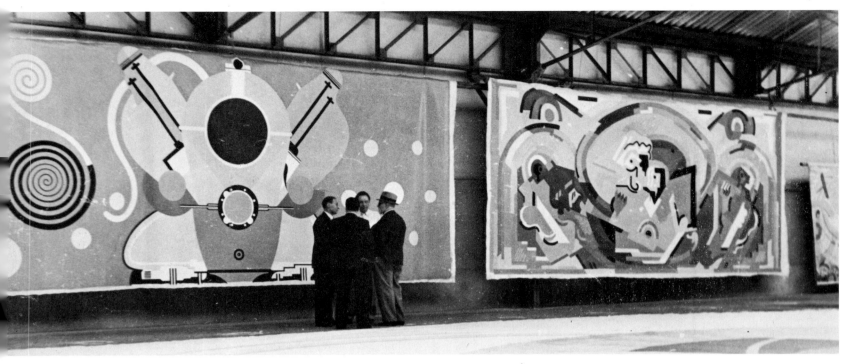

The 1937 International Exhibition: Sonia Delaunay's panel *Aero Engine* next to a panel by Albert Gleizes, in the Aeronautical Pavilion.

SONIA DELAUNAY

The aeroplane shall bring you in his beak
the ribbon of the rainbow
and the immaculate compass-rose.
Your amphora is filled from the warmth of our gazes.
The soft tips of your fingers diffuse rays of light,
puzzles, carnivals and village fairs.
The green serpentine of your cigarette
hung from the simultaneist lamp
like a rattlesnake.
Your coloured-feather words
to fill my pillow of memories.
In the mirror of your face
Modern art smiles upon us.
Within the dome of your hat
tamed aeroplanes shall alight.

ISAAC DEL VANDO-VILLAR

The 1937 International Exhibition:
view of the hall of the Railways
Pavilion; at the farther end, Robert
Delaunay's mural *Air, Iron, Water*.

Below: Sonia Delaunay's mural *Portugal*.

Two of Sonia Delaunay's murals for the Aeronautical Pavilion of the 1937 Exhibition.
These are now in the Museum of Monumental Art at Lund.

View from above of the Aeronautical Pavilion, showing
a panel by Gleizes and Sonia Delaunay's mural *Propeller*

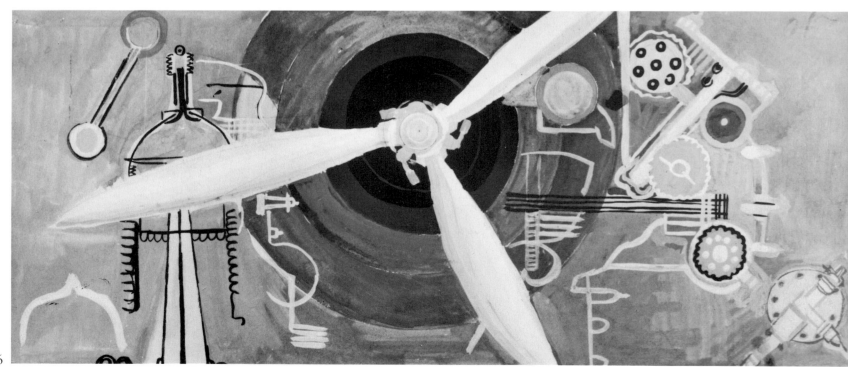

Design for a ceiling for the 1937 Exhibition (never executed).

Sonia Delaunay and Henri Matisse in the Levallois garage-workshop, with her mural *Control Panel* for the Aeronautical Pavilion.

1938 and After

1938 and after

Two artistic events marked 1938 for the Delaunays. Gleizes, who had a hall at the Salon d'Automne at his disposal, invited them to participate with him. Then Othon Friesz asked them to do several large panels, with the help of Gleizes, Villon and Lhote, at the Salon des Tuileries. The Delaunays each executed a vast sixteen foot by sixteen foot canvas for this exhibition.

In 1939 Robert Delaunay founded Réalités Nouvelles, a group whose aim was to bring together all abstract artists. Fredo Sidès, an antique dealer, was its president and Nelly Van Doesburg its secretary. Réalités Nouvelles held its first Salon that year at the Charpentier gallery. This exhibition, as well as the publication of books, and other events, served to counteract the dominating influence of Surrealism. The next important exhibition entirely given over to abstract art was the second Salon des Réalités Nouvelles, held after the war at the Maeght gallery; here the principal works were by Arp and Magnelli.

At the outbreak of the Second World War the Delaunays left for Auvergne, from where they made their way down to the South of France. In 1941, Robert Delaunay, who had been ill for three years, was to die in Montpellier.

The exhibition 'Six artistes à Grasse', held at the Musée Fragonard, Grasse, in 1967, gave Magnelli, Gabrielle Buffet-Picabia and Sonia Delaunay the opportunity to recall this period of their lives.

Magnelli wrote in the catalogue: 'The Delaunays also came down to the South. One day, in Cannes, I was sitting waiting for my wife outside a café just in front of the railway station, when there suddenly appeared a large car packed full of heavy rolls of canvas; who did I see inside it but the Delaunays! We all gestured wildly in greeting. They immediately parked and came to join me at the café to celebrate their arrival and our chance meeting.

'They managed to find a flat at Mougins, and, as we were all staying within a relatively small radius of each other, we had no difficulty in meeting frequently. The first time we went to visit them at Mougins, we were met by the most extraordinary sight. Robert Delaunay had unpacked all his rolls of canvases, comprising works from all periods, and he had literally covered all the walls and even the floors with them. In order to pass from one room to the next, there was no other way but to walk over the paintings. We were somewhat abashed, but Delaunay assured us that it did them no harm at all to walk on them. The effect of this fantastic Delaunay museum was indeed astounding.

'We often met, accompanied by the Arps who lived even closer to us. In fact Arp made his first plaster sculpture in our garden. There he was, scraping away, endlessly repeating: "That's Goering, that's for Goering, I'm scraping Goering's belly".

'Although this was unoccupied France, the Alpes-Maritimes was a poor region, and soon supplies began to run short.

'After Robert Delaunay's death, Sonia came back to Grasse. . . . His death was a great loss for art as well as for his friends. In spite of her grief, and with all of us around to comfort her, she started working once more and undertook a series of gouaches. These, although small, displayed extreme rigour of composition and magnificent luminosity, with an interplay of cold and warm tints — works of undeniable depth and intensity. . . .

'We exchanged works, for in those difficult times we had
254 practically become each other's only clients and collectors. Then

the Arps were given the opportunity to return to Switzerland before the arrival of the Italian troops; the loss of those dear friends narrowed our small circle. Sonia Delaunay and we continued living a life more and more fraught with difficulties — particularly after the Italian armistice, when the Germans took their place. Then it was our turn, and, regretfully, we were obliged to leave La Ferrage where we had lived. For us, this was the end of Grasse, La Ferrage, the Café Bianchi and all that had made our lives there; our story continues, but elsewhere. Nevertheless, the memory of our group and of the bonds of friendship which we formed there, have never left us.'

Gabrielle Buffet-Picabia writes: 'These artists of Grasse take me back to the memory of those dismal years between 1940 and 1943. My section of the Resistance sometimes sent me on missions around Cannes. As often as possible I used to push on a little further — never for very long, alas — to this haven of peace and artistic activity which, through love and work, the small group had succeeded in keeping well away from the chaos that reigned everywhere.

'"During the unreal, dark years of 1940 and 1941, for Sophie Taeuber, Sonia Delaunay, Susi and Alberto Magnelli and myself, Reality and Beauty were our only consolation," writes Jean Arp.

'Profoundly stricken by the death of her husband, Sonia Delaunay had been invited by the Arps to join them at Grasse. They were living at Château-Folie, a beautiful villa in the midst of olive trees whose murmuring foliage (according to Arp) announced the Mistral before one even felt it. It had a magnificent view which stretched over the countryside right down to the Mediterranean.

255

'The beauty of the countryside, the daily meetings at the home of the one or the other, happily took their minds off anxiety and even hunger. The very isolation of their small group created an atmosphere which lent itself to work, and indeed this was for them all a period of intense creative activity; Magnelli's collages and numerous series of paintings, Sonia Delaunay's gouaches and Jean Arp's Mediterranean sculptures, *papiers froissés* and marble and wood reliefs, all date from this period.

'Although the individual style of each is easily distinguishable, nonetheless, the works which were done by Sonia Delaunay and Jean Arp, or by Sonia Delaunay and Magnelli in collaboration, are remarkably coherent and powerful both in colour and in composition. These might easily have been destroyed in the 1944 bombing of the Côte d'Azur, but Sonia Delaunay was able to save them, and it is therefore thanks to her that they could be published after the war. . . .

'Left alone at Grasse — for new threats had dispersed the other members of the group — Sonia Delaunay managed to place in safety all the paintings and sculptures done during this period of relative calm. She started by packing into crates the paintings and personal belonging which they had left at Mougins when, because of Robert Delaunay's illness, they had been forced to leave in a hurry. Then, after the Arps' departure for Switzerland and Sophie Taeuber-Arp's death there, she packed up their belongings too. Finally, she did the same for the Magnellis when they hurriedly left for Paris. Her greatest worry was to save from the bombing the numerous crates of paintings done by her husband, her friends and herself. She in fact succeeded in protecting everything under bags of plaster in the garage under the house.'

Sonia Delaunay liked Grasse, and particularly the view she had from her window at the Grand Hotel, overlooking the old part of the town; she did several drawings of it. When the hotel was taken over by the Italian army, she moved to the Arps' villa about two miles from Grasse. Finding the place too gloomy, however, she managed to obtain another room at the hotel in spite of the military occupation. She recalls how at seven o'clock one morning: 'I was witness to the surrender of two hundred officers holding their arms above their heads, to three Germans who had arrived on motor-bikes. The Italian armistice had recently been signed. I remember seeing a tremendous heap of shells just under my window. . . . The owners of the hotel, who were English, had rented a villa to which I finally moved, and where I remained until I left Grasse in 1944.'

In 1945 all the companions of the Grasse days, excepting Sophie Taeuber-Arp who had tragically died, met up again.

Composition.
...38. Gouache on paper.
...0 × 147 cm; no. 138.
...udy for the painting
...hibited at the Salon d'Automne.
...ivate collection, Paris.

Colour-Rhythm.
1939. Oil on canvas.
158 × 154 cm; no. 1076.
Exhibited at the first Salon
des Réalités Nouvelles, 1939.
Musée de Lille.

Sonia Delaunay 39

260

Composition.
1938. On the left: gouache on paper, 105 × 74,9 cm.
On the right: the monumental version, 5 × 5 m,
done for the Salon des Tuileries, 1938.
Musée Municipal d'Art Moderne, Paris.

Sonia Delaunay and Jean Arp
'Simultaneous' Composition
Lithograph. Grasse, 1942

At Château-Folie, Grasse, in 1942:
Nelly Van Doesburg, Sonia Delaunay,
Sophie Taeuber-Arp and Jean Arp.

Grasse Landscape.
1942. Drawing. 30 × 24 cm; no. 824a.

263

Colour-Rhythm.
Grasse, 1942.
Gouache on paper.
16.8 × 10.2 cm; no. 269.
Private collection, Paris.

Colour-Rhythm.
Paris, 1943.
Watercolour on paper.
28.3 × 21 cm; no. 281.
Private collection, Paris.

Sonia Delaunay 43 - 2#

266

Coloured Rhythms. Paris, 1946. Oil on canvas. 16.6 × 12.8 cm; no. 648a.

Coloured Rhythms. Paris, 1948. Gouache on paper. 81 × 64.5 cm; no. 124a.

268

Coloured Rhythms. Paris, 1949. Gouache on paper. 69.5 × 57.2 cm; no. 339. Private collection, Basle.

269

Coloured Rhythms. 1946. Oil on canvas. 175 × 150 cm; no. 1155. Private collection, New York.

270

Lithograph from the Pagani album. Milan, 1962. 70 × 50 cm.

Composition.
Paris, 1951.
Oil on canvas.
130 × 81 cm; no. 502.
This work obtained
the Lissone Prize.

Colour-Rhythm. 1953. Gouache on paper. 51 × 49.5 cm; no. 9.

Colour-Rhythm. 1950. Gouache on paper; 47.5 × 47 cm; no. 125a. Private collection, Copenhagen.

The Art of Movement

At the time of the 1924 Salon d'Automne, Robert Delaunay wrote an account of his wife's contribution to the show:

'When Baudelaire wrote his famous: *"Je hais le mouvement qui déplace les lignes"* (I hate movement which displaces lines), he could not foresee that a time would come when both artists and poets would place above all else forms in movement. One of the attractions of the 1924 Salon d'Automne is the exhibition of cinematic "simultaneous" materials. Simultaneity — what does this concept really mean ?

'As you stroll among the boutiques proliferating in the vast hall of the Grand Palais, something different draws you to the boutique decorated with Madame Sonia Delaunay's materials: Everything seems to be in movement there. The first impact on the retina has the appeal of the unexpected. But then your mind reacts and seeks to understand. The effect is reinforced by the other boutiques nearby which you cannot help but see; they create a contrast which makes you feel as if transported into the static world of the Musée Grevin — no doubt an important event in Naturalist history! What brings about this change, how to explain this state of things? Naturally, we are not even referring to all these dead, static paintings hung all over the Exhibition. Does this not compare well with the first chapter of a novel by Delteil? that's it: *La peste à Paris dans les cinq sens.* But in Delteil there is life, there is intrinsic movement.

'We find in Madame Sonia Delaunay a projection of the inner self which is nowhere better or more vividly illustrated than in her fabric design. She has linked this poetry of colour in manifold rhythms, multiplied fivefold by varying "simultaneous" speeds — by this we mean rhythms controlled by her own

274

masterly intuition. Up till then, cinematic art had been limited to a play of successive photographic cut-outs, by which they tried to give a semblance of real life. This was a poor and restricted means, for even the best colour photography cannot equal the effect you gain through bathing in an impressionist atmosphere at the right temperature. Madame Delaunay's boutique gives you an idea of what a live and controlled spectacle could be: made to measure just for you.

'The pattern of proportions in the artist's work is manifold and changing, as for example in the thirteen- by ten-foot window display which Apollinaire already called "the art of window-dressing." She has invented a device of rolls unrolling which offer the onlooker a show of infinite "simultaneous" variations of coloured forms depicting poets and sights of Paris. The device can be set up vertically, as originally designed, or as at the Salon d'Automne, shooting out in all directions. It can also be used to create action behind the backs of the actors.

'I shall never forget the first time I saw Cendrars' poem the *Transsibérien* with its composite, wild, living colour-rhythms. Today poetry can be projected not only in one, but in all directions, facilitating the transmission of new messages to people who seldom have the opportunity to read.'

Sonia Delaunay has since given her own view of her work:

'One needs to re-learn to paint — and in order to do so, discover new methods, new technical and sculptural methods.

'Colour, freed from its descriptive, literary use, must be grasped as such, in its own particular richness.

'The subject is of no importance; it can be hinted at, or else arise out of the coloured configuration itself.

'He who knows how to appreciate colour relationships, the influence of one colour on another, their contrasts and dissonances, is promised an infinitely diverse imagery.

'With colour comes the essential structural element of rhythm, which is movement based on numbers.

'Just as, in written poetry, that which counts is not the mere juxtaposition of words but the act of creation mysteriously provoking (or not provoking) emotion; so in colours, what counts is the poetry, the mysterious inner vitality — emanating and communicating. At last, we have hopes of a new language.

'I am against the introduction of literature into the plastic arts. To my mind, the poetry emanating from a work of art must be born out of lyricism expressed by purely plastic means. Any foreign element grafted on to these is proof of inadequate craftsmanship and represents a most regrettable error. Neither Mondrian nor Robert Delaunay needed to resort to literature to attain poetic expressivity in their works.

'One must preserve a spontaneous contact with one's inner self. Painting must never degenerate into habit. An artist is constantly working, even when he is not in front of his easel. And each time he does paint, he must seek to express some new idea — or rather, his effort must result in a more perfect rendering of what he is trying to express throughout his life. It is the antithesis of modern mass production, the canker of our society. Such must be the viewpoint of the artist who does not need to discriminate between technique and aesthetics since both lead to a single issue, the poetry of colour.'

The prime importance of movement for our understanding of
Sonia Delaunay's work has been most aptly analysed by Bernard

Dorival in his foreword to the Sonia and Robert Delaunay exhibition held in Canada in 1965:

'But they reveal also a more ambitious artistic aspiration. This aspiration is clearly seen in their desire to reinstate in painting the movement and colour the orthodox Cubists had banished; the latter had most probably done this because it was the easier alternative. Foreshadowing the Italian Futurists, the Delaunays and their colleagues exalted the dynamic aspects of modern life, inventing new ways to express movement. Take for instance La Fresnaye's *Artillery*, Villon's *Soldiers on the Move*, Gleizes' *Football Players*, Robert Delaunay's *Cardiff Team*, or Sonia Delaunay's *Bal Bullier*. They also refused to restrict their palette to the greys, ochres and dull greens so dear to Picasso and Braque, and returned to light, bright and strong tints which could best express atmosphere and luminosity in the case of Villon and La Fresnaye, and best express the immensity of the universe and the powerfulness of life in the case of the Delaunays.'

Coloured Rhythms. 1952. Gouache on paper. 56 × 76 cm; no. 172. Musée National d'Art Moderne, Paris.

Coloured Rhythms. 1954. Gouache on paper. 87 × 57.5 cm; no. 166.

Composition.
1955-1958. Oil on canvas. 158 × 215 cm.
Musée National d'Art Moderne, Paris.
This is one of the masterpieces of this period.

Coloured Rhythms. Grasse, 1942. Gouache on paper. 24.5 × 20.2 cm; no. 223a. Private collection, Paris.

RHYTHM
is the regulation of
    MOVEMENT
      Plato

Who is the artist
for whom
the perfectly straight LINE
or the perfect CIRCLE
has any value?

When we speak
of the line are we not
implying its own special way
of betraying STRAIGHTNESS?

Colour-Rhythm.
1942. Gouache on paper.
20 × 19.5 cm; no. 329.
Private collection, New York.

MAGIC of the sign, of form,
magic of rhythm.
ETERNAL MARK OF THE PRESENT.
'A work of art is required
both to conceal and reveal
at one and the same time
the presence of its creator.'
All the interest lies in the
REVELATION.

ALL
great works
are static, simple,
mysterious,
profoundly, incalculably
EVOCATIVE, even when
their external appearance seems
limited to the present day.
STATICS is the BALANCE
of forces. The emotional
power which emanates from
this balance of values is the
DYNAMICS
of all art.

Colour-Rhythm. 1947. Gouache. 76 × 56 cm; no. 779. Private collection, Florence.

Forms are
SITES.
The idea of their orientation
GOVERNS the sites and the
networks of construction are
unexpectedly complex.

That which we call place,
imaginary space, comes from a
grasping of the real which tries not to
TRANSCRIBE nature
but to order, to compose
the nexus revealed, to set up
an ensemble.
The artist magnetizes,
transforms SPACE,
defines his terms, the various
states of passion, characterizes
the actions, examining
not the ends but the MEANS.

'The art that is most DYNAMIC
is that where the laws of
STATICS
are respected and put to
the best aesthetic use.'

286

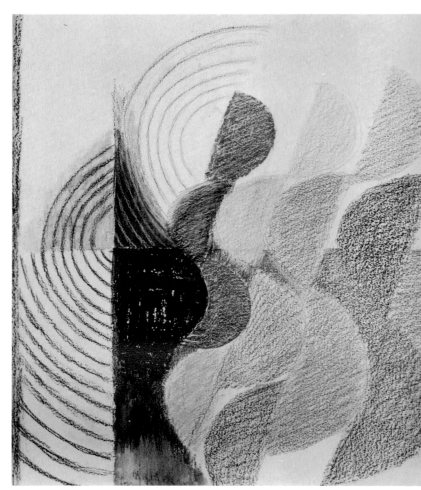

Between reality, nature,
heavenly bodies, imaginary space,
the distance has never been very
GREAT. But the disproportion
and not the distinction — which is
an elementary phenomenon —
distance and force set up
a difference of potential at the
limits. These limits are bodied forth

in places, attributes whose
power is
IMMENSE.
There is a magic of MAGNETISM
which comes after the disappearance of the
sense of prophecy. But its survival in
us, in the work of art, is THAT
CONFLICT
between occult learning

and the artist's authority,
between the initiate and the spectator
(blind, and yet he has his say)
between the CURIOSITY and
the RESISTANCE
that one feels in the presence of LOST
LORE or the laws of renewal.
This is one of the
sources of great ART.

Initial studies for *Composition* (reproduced pp. 280-281).
1951. Pencil on paper. 32 × 23.5 cm; no. 246.
1955. 'Primolo' crayons on paper; 56 × 49 cm; no. 541.
1953. Etching in dry-point for the Schwarz album, Milan.

288

Composition for *Jazz*. Second series. 1952. Gouache on paper, 77 × 57 cm; no. 336.

'Calculated FORMS and just space bring to life

a thousand magical, prompt and molten lives.'

'common ideas
INVOLVED
in differing proportions
serve as a link,
to bring together
the other things
to which they were severally
ATTACHED.'

289

Colour-Rhythm on Black. 1948. Oil on canvas. 11.4 × 44.5 cm; no. 616.

What COLOURS paper
is the mind in action,
at boiling-point. A response,
a noise, a movement,
an impact which are the instant
and simultaneous effects of
our impressions change
colour every instant.

And even the purest of forms will
NEVER STAY THE SAME.

Colour-Rhythm. 1959-1960. Oil on canvas. 130 × 162 cm; no. 894. Kunsthalle, Bielefeld.

Colour-Rhythm.
1950. Gouache.
56.5 × 37.5 cm.
Private collection, Paris.

She channels the fluids,
she seeks out the fenced-off places,
the essential POINTS.
Every rhythm is a
PROPOSITION
which can be made up of others,
and thus we can, without more
thought for sight or for movement,
know the properties of the
COMBINATIONS
presented to us, and
build to enrich
space by means of those
well linked rhythms,
'She draws from the darkness
the whole of its
OPERATIONS.'

BLUE complains, BLACK
sleeps with his eyes wide open,
a YELLOW sweetness descends upon us.
Engrossed, forgetful — where is RED?
On your feet, GREEN! We're
there at last, I've been here since red.
Beautiful, sparkling blue bends,
takes my head in its hands,
and harshly questions me.

The STARS do their
rounds in the sky
tracing arcs of circles
and leaving luminous trails
    which thus manifest the

OBEY
the commandments
of the
    HEART
make the world anew
recreate what we must believe
— even to DENYING death.

One might think oneself
in some sort of LUNA PARK
    inside some
WONDERLAND
moved by a
MAGIC HAND.

The Scallywag ('L'Affreux Jojo'). 1947. Oil on canvas. 207 × 192 cm; no. 1252. Jacques Damase Collection, Paris.

Depth-Rhythm. 1960. Oil on canvas. 130 × 162 cm; no. 898. Musée National d'Art Moderne, Paris.

Forms of silence and lucidity
infinitely calm, infinitely
alert, rigid and
seeming endowed with all of life,
they seem to be
intelligence incarnate piercing
through all things. What is there more
MYSTERIOUS than CLARITY?

Some journeys are beneficial.
Forms are always travelling.
Hardly has the journey been decreed,
than these forms cover
vast distances in
the artist's mind. These forms
do not stop, but their
PRESENCE
is such that they are never forgotten.

That one holds my hand,
and yet is coloured from elsewhere.
This one, look at it from close to
and already it is far away.
One remote, the other IMMENSE,
How shall we ever tell
which is the most real,
MOST
THE   BEAUTIFUL

Colour-Rhythm. Paris, 1958. Oil on canvas; 112 × 192 cm. De Leew Collection, Amsterdam.

Coloured Rhythm. 1948. Gouache. No. 569. Private collection, Paris.

An ARMY of ideas assails her,
well marshalled powerful as
the eclipse, an earthquake.

The true reason why this form departs
is that it wants to be
able to come back. These
alignments, these formations
suggest that the artist must know
the art of the
STRATEGIST.
Bent lines, phalanxes of
fearsome square shoulders,
martial diamonds, figures
essentially SIMPLE.
Yet each portion
of these figures is extremely
COMPLEX.
In the depths of silence
the most complex forms
blend with the most simple,
and those that are identical
summarize and simplify each other.

Colour Poem. Paris, 1960.
Gouache on paper. 22 × 26 cm.
Private collection, Paris.

297

'Thought is
DIV   I   DED
between
construction and cognition.'

A work of art being,
if it has vigour, the
HIGHEST
AFFIRMATION
of a specified personality,
Therefore, it cannot avoid a CLASH
with all other personalities.

'TRUTH in Art,
in the work of art itself, is incorporated
as is
LIFE in the ANIMAL.'

Simultaneous contrasts of colours,
expressive power of coloured harmonies,
unfolding of their abstract possibilities:
penetrating warmth, high-flying lyricism . . .
'All rhythms intermingle,
ALL IS MOVEMENT
in simultaneous colours.'

Colour-Rhythm. 1959. Oil on canvas. 116 × 88 cm; no. 876. Private collection, Turin.

Composition. 1948. Gouache on paper. No. 763. Private collection, Paris.

301

Colour-Rhythm. 1950. Gouache. 56.5 × 37.5 cm. Private collection, Paris.

SAMEDI 3 OCTORRE 1959

Colour-Rhythm. Paris, 1959. Gouache on paper. 54 × 35 cm. Private collection, Paris.

Colour and Dynamism

Sonia Delaunay has always been guided more by her intrinsic good taste and her sensitivity than by any specific and definable aesthetic theory.

Already as an adolescent, she had been fascinated by the harmonies and contrasts of colours. When she met Robert Delaunay, she was going through a phase of uncertainty and doubt, seeking to break through the limitations of drawing without being able to replace it by any structure that would be both autonomous and quite different. Robert Delaunay's *Simultaneous Contrasts* — those bright colour constructions for which he had a genius — taught her to break through this barrier. Conversely, as we saw in the *Market in the Minho*, it was she who helped Robert Delaunay to solve the problem of light.

The early research undertaken by the Delaunays coincided in fact with the very heights of Cubism. Their contribution to the art of their times was nevertheless considerable, as Pierre Francastel has stressed:

'Cézanne had broken the vase, and it was not enough just to bring the pieces together again or even simply show up the broken fragments. A new purpose for art had to be found, which did more than merely translate on to canvas or through plastic means a series of visual paper cut-outs, or succeeding segments of reality, corresponding to the comfortable visual habits of society as a whole. . . . Delaunay has understood, as had his wife and Gleizes (who was one of the first to recognize his genius), that art, in the century of the wave-motion theory, required a new way of apprehending visual perception.'

Both the Delaunays refused the influence of Cubism and its conceptual abstractions, aiming to overcome the inertia of flat

Encounter. 1959.
Gouache on paper. 56 × 39 cm.
Jacques Damase Collection, Paris.

planes by the creation of 'simultaneous' surfaces radiating colour and light. From the first Sonia had been interested in the artistic properties of different materials and, with her book-covers, had studied the possibilities of 'integrating different arts'.

The study of movement resulted in watercolours, often heightened with coloured pencils, such as the *Dancer, 109* of 1916. In this work, the figure of the dancer is almost abstract, and is suggested by a diagonal coil which in its turn engenders discs painted in cold tones. These stand out against 'simultaneous' coloured circles, the whole work conjuring forth continuous rhythms. The *Spanish Dancer* of 1917 is both more elaborate and more representational, and yet allows the colours to open out freely. A haunting theme made of spheres, segments and arcs runs through each composition; each rhythm takes it up, passes it on to the next until it reaches a point where time and space are united.

If at times her work became less abstract — for instance during her Hispano-Portuguese period, in some self-portraits, in the *Journeys Far Away* of 1937 and in the *Apples* painted at Grasse in 1943 — nonetheless, the subject was totally changed; it abandoned the contingent world, and took upon itself a stern reality. Despite a narrow technical 'vocabulary', pure colours and stringent discipline, her works still have the power to effect our emotions. Thickly spread reds merge with blues in a burst of lyricism where colours and forms generate and complete each other in the very act of movement; a latent dynamism gives tension and structure to the work.

There is not the slightest trace of monotony, despite the apparent narrowness of her artistic repertory, for a rhythmic power is incorporated in her works and becomes the vehicle of a permanent discovery. Violence is overcome, and the artist, by elaborating her apprehension of space and time, projects and actualizes them through an ambiguously static reality.

While Matisse had used the arabesque to interpret the form of objects, Sonia Delaunay uses abstraction and poetry; a poetry of pure forms and colours, free of all overbearing subjectivism; a poetry as abstract as music and partaking of Rimbaud's and Mallarmé's vision.

She is helped by certain instinctive qualities, her love of life, her youthful attitude and her desire to create.

The art critic Deroudille said: 'It would be interesting to study the contribution of Russian artists to Modern Art. It would enable us to evaluate the Slavonic influence on the rapid evolution of Expressionism. Moreover, one could then ascertain how far their natural tendency towards symbolism and their will to express inner impulses influenced the development of contemporary abstract techniques.'

Robert Delaunay acknowledged the influence that his wife had upon his art thus: 'Coming from the East she brought with her its warmth and mystery. The contact with Occidental ways did not harm it, on the contrary, this tendency was strengthened, finding a new constructive outlet in the very friction between the two manners of being. It widened out, developed, and transformed her art into something new, formally blending Western and Eastern characteristics, so to speak; becoming an indivisible whole of which she alone was the creator.

'Like all artists and poets of the East, she has a hereditary bent for colour. One already feels this lyricism, this need to express herself through colours — dazzling yet still timid and uncertain — in her first studies done on her own or under the supervision of a teacher.' (Quoted by Francastel.)

Sonia Delaunay herself stresses the significance of colour in her art: 'Colour has become an essential means of expression for us, just like speech. We play with colours as if they had recently been invented. A colour on a surface will affect all the neighbouring ones. If it is wrong in relation to the whole, all the others must be altered. The luminous light of Spain and Portugal helped us to understand exactly what differentiates a

colour, what gives it its proper pitch and its individual life.

Colours are like the figures of a poetical language, there to render psychic states [*états d'âme*].

And it was precisely in this field that her contribution to art was the most original.

Orphism was born in 1913 from the researches undertaken by Robert Delaunay and Guillaume Apollinaire. The latter named it after his poem *Bestiaire ou Cortège d'Orphée* because Orpheus' song was said to tame wild beasts and move trees and rocks; by analogy, the rhythmic music of Orphism sought to sweep along in its wake all recalcitrant objects. Robert Delaunay wrote: 'Pure colour translating the rhythm is often laid in complete or segmented concentric circles which disclose the whole spectrum of the prism, creating a violent dazzling effect. The vortex thus obtained radiates and gives life to such works — while never forgetting that this is a work of decoration.'

Though faithful to the tenets of Orphism, Sonia Delaunay also appears to have been aware of the decorative significance of painting. Her murals and monumental tapestries won her the respect of present-day partisans of functionalism, for whom the primary role of painting is to 'clothe' an architecture as it had done in many great monuments of the past.

Each of Sonia Delaunay's paintings is a lyrical colour poem. Her chromatic dynamism reaches supreme heights of exaltation in works apparently simple, clear and precise; moreover, the painful effort of elaboration never shows through. In his book *Jubilations,* Akaim Volynski wrote a chapter entitled 'Straight Lines and Curved Lines'. The latter contains a fascinating philosophical analysis of certain geometrical concepts, which serves to shed light on Sonia Delaunay's art:

'Every line has its own logic and psychology. The straight line is infinite, in both directions; it is the constant motion of a point in the same direction, tending towards its end. Let us imagine a straight line drawn on a blackboard. Does it not give us the impression of a violent, if not magic, constraint imposed upon reality where curved and closed lines predominate? If we were to illustrate our thought process through a plastic medium, we would obtain a geometrical straight line, regular and clear-cut, endlessly going towards its end, yet drowned in the impersonal chaotic darkness of its surroundings.

'The zigzag line is a composite variant of the straight line. It is the symbol of the man who constantly changes his targets in life. Basically we still have the same magic straight line, the same movement of the luminous point through obscure space, the same precipitation of thought over chaos and precipices. . . . But its buckled form harbours a wealth of complicated elements. Man is forever seduced by the most diverse ends; and, in his attempt to attain what he takes for truth, he embarks on the most varied courses. . . . At every moment discrepancies between reality and the chosen ideal arise, and are translated into painful and arduous zigzags. It is along these zigzags that the lives of outstanding men are often played — and few manage to accomplish their journey without straying from the straight course they have set themselves.

'And what of the curved line? It is one drawn by a mobile point which, under the pressure of external forces, constantly deviates from its rectilineal course. Now, this is exactly how life superficially appears to be — each object influencing and adapting the other, but itself subjected to the influence of its surroundings. Here all is chaos and confusion. Instead of aspiring towards an end, all things converge upon themselves, here, the momentum is no longer given by thought but by will-power. The clash of individual wills and a thousand and one sentimental motivations make up the world of open or closed curved lines in their infinite kaleidoscopic diversity.'

The Delaunays' most original pictorial contribution lay in their colour; but, as this quotation serves to remind us, another element inseparable from their art is that of movement.

Coloured Rhythms. 1959. Gouache on paper. 56 × 76 cm; no. 881. Private collection, Oslo.

Colour-Rhythm. 1959. Oil on canvas. 161 × 130 cm; no. 878. Private collection, Paris.

The Donation

After Georges Braque, Robert and Sonia Delaunay were the first artists to see their own works at the Louvre. In 1964, a hundred and thirteen works of both artists were exhibited in the great hall of the Pavillon Mollien, and Sonia Delaunay was thus able to see the result of fifty years of work, on show in the same building that housed the paintings of Leonardo and Rembrandt.

Before the War, Robert Delaunay had already thought of founding an art gallery on their estate at Gambais, Ile de France. (The project was more than a dream, for Le Corbusier had even begun sketching a few designs for it.) It would have been the first Museum of Modern Art in the Ile de France. It was a good plan, as is all decentralization in matters of art, and was in keeping with the ideas of both the Delaunays.

Jean Cassou, chief curator of the Musée National d'Art Moderne, introduced the Louvre exhibition thus, on 8 February 1964:

'The Louvre presents, in the exhibition hall of the Pavillon Mollien, the donation recently made to the Musée National d'Art Moderne by Madame Sonia Delaunay, widow of Robert Delaunay and herself a talented artist. This donation comprises sixteen paintings by Robert Delaunay and twelve by Sonia Delaunay, plus a large number of other works by both artists using different media and techniques such as reliefs, mosaics, paintings on cement, *papiers collés,* book-covers, materials and so on.

'In this collection of works — so varied, so vehemently and passionately alive — Robert and Sonia Delaunay seem to us still as close to each other, as united, as they were during their lives and in the course of their careers as artists.

'Sonia Delaunay's role during this admirable and truly significant dual career is particularly praiseworthy. Robert Delaunay's genius was unique, yet at the same time, one must speak of Robert and Sonia Delaunay and must constantly associate them in a common activity. In the domain of fabrics and fashions, Sonia — sometimes alone and sometimes in collaboration with Robert — was able to show us the existence of a Cubist style — meaning that Cubism was not only an aesthetic doctrine but also a manner of thinking and of feeling, capable of manifesting itself in everyday objects. . .

'While her husband was still alive, Sonia discreetly kept in the background as a painter, expressing herself in the marvellous decorative works which have indeed contributed to establish her own reputation.

'After Robert Delaunay's early death (for he was only fifty-six when he died), she returned to painting, determined to keep alive her husband's artistic message as much in her works as in her teaching.

'She gathered around her enthusiastic pupils and at the same time devoted herself to creative work of increasing intensity, applying her profound understanding of the prismatic play of light to achieve new dazzling developments.

'Madame Sonia Delaunay's generous gift is a priceless acquisition to the Musée National d'Art Moderne and demonstrates in a striking manner the importance of Robert Delaunay, and equally that of the duo Robert and Sonia Delaunay, in the artistic panorama of our century.'

It is also thanks to Sonia Delaunay that the Musée National d'Art Moderne gained the Brancusi collection. Brancusi did not get on very well with Robert Delaunay — just as he did not get on with most people – but when Sonia returned to Paris in 1944, she looked him up and thereafter saw him fairly often:

'When I began seeing more of Brancusi, he was already a wise elder, diffusing an aura of spiritual peace which helped one live through one's anxieties.

'He had become a marvellous old man, full of life, with keen black eyes and white hair, and always dressed in white overalls. He was a great artist, but at the same time he always remained a great craftsman, with an exacting sense of professionalism, which was truly exceptional. Everything had to pass through his own hands. This was the essential quality which set him apart from the artists of his epoch.

'Our own passion for our art, Delaunay's and mine, and our own exacting demands both in research and in creation, drew us to Brancusi. Therefore, when one day he told me how worried he was about the fate of his works after his death, and how he would have liked his studio to be preserved just as it was with his works still in place, and for it all to be given to the French nation, it occured to me that our friend Jean Cassou, chief curator of the Musée National d'Art Moderne, might be able to help him. I contacted Cassou, and soon after we both paid Brancusi a visit. Brancusi had never taken French nationality, and did not feel up to taking the necessary steps, so, for four years, Georges Salles and Jean Cassou did all in their power to realize the project. Finally, Brancusi's studio was reconstructed (his real studio having had to be demolished) inside the Museum.

'When I used to visit him, he always offered to fetch champagne out of the fridge. He also always recounted the same stories of how he had arrived in Paris on foot, of how he had travelled to Florence in the company of Raymond Radiguet, and many other wonderful tales. At the end of his life he became very influenced by Hindu mysticism. He became more and more distressed by the fact that after his death his works might be sent back to Romania, the country of his birth.

'As far as my modest means allowed me, I did all I could to help safeguard this life's-work and bring about the success of our project. I am very happy to have been instrumental in realizing the wishes of my old friend Brancusi.'

O MADAME SONIA DELAUNAY

olitude covered with so much snow
ho then has rent the skin of these mirrors
nder the eye of Time poets ripen
t us slightly change the direction of leaning seas
he storm can no longer be held back
he captain puts in his spare lungs.

have nothing left but void under seal
nd folded void

he big circus snakes
ave smiled on the tropic

nalaise
f Time devoured by vermin

oh, why was Magellan not killed at Nice
by the eclipse?

Ear with cornets of air
dead for so many years
the shoulders of the seas
with seaweed kisses

No seagull this morning has cried out: LAND.

B. FONDANE

Colour-Rhythm. Paris, 1958.
Oil on canvas. 100 × 80 cm.
Private collection, Genoa.

Sonia Delaunay photographed at Bielefeld in 1959.

317

Black Squares. Lithograph, 1968; 65 × 50 cm.

Colour-Rhythm. 1959. Oil on canvas. 116×88 cm; no. 877. Private collection, Copenhagen.

High-warp tapestry made
at the Gobelins factory.
1966-1967. 280 × 410 cm.
Mobilier National, Paris.

322

Colour-Rhythm. 1965. Gouache on paper. 52 × 39 cm; no. 1302.

SD 67

Colour-Rhythm. 1967. Oil on canvas. 200 × 150 cm; no. 1554.

324

Colour-Rhythm. 1964. Gouache on paper; 78 × 56.5 cm; no. 1146. Jacques Damase Collection, Paris.

Rhythm. 1956. Oil on canvas. 116 × 88 cm; no. 555. Museo di Locarno, Arp donation.

326

Colour-Rhythm. 1967. Gouache on paper. 57 × 38 cm; no. 1457. Private collection, Munich.

327

Ellipse. 1969. Gouache on paper. 78 × 57 cm; no. 1606. Private collection, Turin.

Colour-Rhythm.
1962. Gouache.
56.4 × 73.5 cm; no. 959a.
Private collection, Los Angeles.

Colour-Rhythm. 1964. Gouache on paper. 78 × 56.5 cm; no. 1149. Rothschild collection, New York.

Colour-Rhythm. 1956. Gouache and black pencil. 34 × 48 cm; no. 542. Private collection, London.

331

Colour-Rhythm, after a poem by Rimbaud.
1961. Gouache on paper. 67 × 50.5 cm; no. 960.
Private collection, Paris.

Colour-Rhythm.
1961. Gouache on paper.
65 × 48 cm; no. 920.
Musée National d'Art Moderne, Paris.

Colour-Rhythm.
1965. Gouache on paper. 28.5 × 23 cm; no. 1268.

Colour-Rhythm.
1965. Gouache on paper. 19 × 10 cm; no. 1264.
Private collection, Paris.

Colour-Rhythm. 1967. Oil on canvas. 125 × 250 cm; no. 1532.

Colour-Rhythm. 1968. Oil on canvas. 92 × 72 cm; no. 1579. Private collection, Belgium.

Triptych. 1963. Oil on canvas. 100 × 200 cm; no. 1052. Tate Gallery, London.

Colour-Rhythm. 1964. Oil on canvas. 96.5 × 194 cm; no. 1148.

Colour-Rhythm. 1967. Oil on canvas. 225 cm diameter; no. 1541.

Colour-Rhythm. 1967. Gouache on paper. 60 × 53 cm; no. 1491. Musée du Havre

342

our-Rhythm. 1969. Oil on canvas. 130 × 97 cm; no. 1633.
sented to Richard M. Nixon by Georges Pompidou when the latter visited the United States in 1970.

Colour-Rhythm. 1960. Gouache on cardboard. 58 × 56 cm. Dimona Museum, Israel.

Sonia Delaunay in her studio in 1967, in front of a *Colour-Rhythm* painting of 1962.

Graphic Art

347

Cover of Canudo's book *Les Transplantés*. 1913. Collage of materials. 26 × 17 cm; no. 642.

Graphic Art

Being so aware of the problems of her times, it was to be expected that Sonia Delaunay should take an active interest in graphic research. Her essentially visual sensibility had, in the course of her artistic career, always led her to transform into works of art all that surrounded her.

Struck by the beauty and the novelty of Cendrars' poem *Pâques à New York* which he had read to the Delaunays the first time he had visited them, she had immediately set about binding it in suede with a *papier-collé* design on the outside. The fly-leaves were made up of great coloured squares, which influenced Klee.

This was a starting-point. Subsequently she did the covers for the bound annual volumes of the periodical *Der Sturm* and for the works of many poets and novelists such as Rimbaud, Apollinaire, Laforgue, Canudo and Jourdan.

Then came the famous book published in collaboration with Cendrars: *La Prose du Transsibérien et de la petite Jehanne de France*, in which revolutionary composition, original typography and text blended into one. The poem was later to be named the 'incunabulum of the twentieth century'.

Sonia Delaunay's poster-poems, a form later to be exploited by Dada, also date from this period. The first of these, based on Cendrars's *Zenith*, was exhibited at the Berlin Herbstsalon of 1913; its origin was an advertisement devised by Blaise Cendrars for Zenith watches in the hope of earning a little money — however, he forgot to propose his idea to the firm. The text ran as follows: 'Record time! Midday strikes on its solar anvil the beams of Zenith light.'

This was followed by many other poster-poems: sketches for Pirelli tyres, a richly coloured poster for Dubonnet and projects

for Pernod, Linel colour pencils and the particularly successful luminous 'Zig-Zag', which was awarded the first prize at a competition organized by the Compagnie Parisienne d'Electricité. She made extensive use of paper cut-outs in designing her posters. The striking simplicity and the typographical neatness of these works — in those days considered far too audacious — have influenced many famous poster designers, including the celebrated Cassandre. The harmonious combination of colours is often obtained through the juxtaposition of neighbouring shades, for instance vermilion and brick-red, vermilion and pink, ultramarine and bright blue. The subjects of the posters are barely suggested; and these are more often than not completely abstract — granting of course that letters are abstractions. The importance of the Dubonnet and Zenith cut-outs is undeniable, and as Michel Hoog stresses: 'They are not to be connected with contemporary Cubist *papiers collés,* nor with the Surrealist collages. Rather, they prefigure Matisse's large paper cut-outs.'

At least twenty years before Matisse, Sonia Delaunay was directly 'drawing in colour' — instead of drawing a preliminary outline to be filled in with colours. This simplification of two stages into one guarantees extreme precision; this was no tentative beginning, but the result of research.

In *Zone,* she went even further and made the letters so abstract that they became sheer rhythm. This particular work takes us back to the *Pâques* and the early days of the Delaunays' friendship with Apollinaire. The latter had had the idea of founding a periodical to be called *Zone;* this was also the title of one of his poems which, according to Tristan Tzara, had been inspired by a hearing of Cendrars's *Pâques à New York.* Sonia Delaunay's design for *Zone* most probably influenced Lissitzky in his use of the diagonal in graphic compositions.

The preparation for the 1925 Decorative Arts Exhibition, the vast murals for the 1937 Exhibition, and many other preoccupations supervened, and Sonia Delaunay abandoned this type of work. She only returned to it after Robert Delaunay's death. In 1942, in collaboration with Arp, Magnelli and Sophie Taeuber-Arp, she created a strange but fascinating album where each lithograph was the combined work of two artists: Sonia Delaunay and Arp, Sonia Delaunay and Magnelli, etc.

After the Liberation, many writers, including Maurice Raynal and André Salmon, asked her to do the covers of their books. André Bloc asked her to contribute to *L'Art d'aujourd'hui*. She did a series of lithographs for the Milan publisher Pagani, a set of enormous *pochoirs* for an album published by Denise René, and a number of etchings in colour for Arturo Schwarz.

For her old friend Tristan Tzara, she did four gouaches to be reproduced in *pochoir* in his *Fruit permis* in 1956, and also coloured engravings for *Juste présent* in 1961.

Among many others, one should also mention various catalogue covers, invitation cards, posters for her own exhibitions (the Bielefeld exhibition, for instance) — all of which were worked and reworked until they reached perfection. For one of her grandsons, just learning to read, she began a marvellous *Alphabet* which was ultimately published by Emme Edizioni of Milan in 1969.

In 1964 she completed a set of playing-card designs commissioned by the curator of the Kunsthalle, Bielefeld. (In 1938 she had already had the idea, and had even begun sketching a few cards.) The court cards were conceived in such a way that they express the essential nature of the figure represented rather than its meaning, traditionally conveyed by ornaments, emblems and symbols. Thus the figure of the king expresses virility by means of large, static rhomboidal forms; the femininity of the queen is characterized by rounded, mobile forms; the jack is distinguished from both by its restlessness, its playful agility, its boyishness. The headgear is the only traditional emblem maintained, and quite deliberately so, for after all the pack of cards is an object intended for use, and not simply to satisfy the eye. As for the two jokers, Sonia Delaunay used as a basic design, but in a more abstract fashion, the first *Jazz* compositions done in 1952. The design used for the backs of the cards is a variation on the traditional harlequin pattern; there are two versions, one in red and blue and the other in green and blue.

The figures of king, queen and jack are identical in each of the four suits of the pack. Further to facilitate the use of the cards, the artist developed a supplementary system of colours; the same colours are used for the twelve cards, but each suit has a different dominant — blue for clubs, green for spades, red for hearts and yellow for diamonds. The remainder of the cards of the pack were also painted by Sonia Delaunay, and the hand-drawn effect remained even when they were reproduced.

There is nothing cold and calculating about these 'simultaneous' cards. Sonia Delaunay disciplined her vitality to create a seemingly straight-forward composition of forms and colours; nonetheless their essential lyricism shows through.

Equally interesting are the motifs, apparently simple, employed by Sonia Delaunay for a set of ceramics; some of these were the fruit of earlier research, but all bear the mark of her personality.

In 1967-68, she once again tackled the integration of letters into a plastic composition when preparing the poster announcing her retrospective exhibition at the Musée National d'Art Moderne.

Mention must be made of her carpets and tapestries. These, to our mind, enter the field of her graphic research.

A carpet must fit into the specific architectural requirements of the floor, which presents a different problem to that of walls. Artists who can truly 'think carpet' are few and far between, and all too often designs, once enlarged and woven, still reflect the art of the painter. Nevertheless, the most gifted artists have always known how to adapt themselves to the specific nature of the problems envisaged and thereby find a logical solution. From 1920-22 and in keeping with her interest in what has since 1925 been termed Decorative Art, Sonia Delaunay applied herself to the design of carpets. She continued her research into rhythms and colours when designing her carpets, in the same way as she had done when designing her materials. The designs for those done during this period for a few art collectors such as Dr. Viard and M. Coutrot, or in collaboration with architects for important decorative projects, have never been reproduced. It was only in 1967 that an edition of her work in this field was undertaken, reproducing, among other more or less recent designs, one of her first carpets executed in 1925. Like her fabric designs, this carpet has still not dated.

The colours of Sonia Delaunay's carpets are in her characteristic range of rich deep resonances and unexpected correspon-

dences; they are a return to true floor architecture, and a new source of light and joy. As always, we are caught up in the spell of the mysterious dynamism of her large rectangles, triangles, squares and discs.

When reproducing her carpets, which were originally hand-woven, she chose a technique used for some of the early fifteenth-century Spanish rugs, which was a medieval technique — the knotted stitch of the Seljuks. Vegetable dyes only were used, which gave an effect of incomparable freshness.

The requirements of the wall, in terms of tapestries, mosaics or stained glass, are again quite different. In all three — in the medium of large tapestries woven at the Gobelins or at Aubusson, in the mosaic walls executed in Italy, in the stained glass windows for a Romanesque chapel in South-West France — Sonia Delaunay solved the particular problem which the medium presented, and adapted her work in consequence. For the stained-glass windows of the Romanesque chapel, she knew how to limit her colour range and simplify as far as possible her figures and rhythms, so that the whole would blend in with the thirteenth-century frescoes decorating the walls. In her tapestries, even if she has re-used certain of the great themes of her recent works, one has to acknowledge that she has successfully combined the large expanses of colour with passages originally treated in crayons and pastels. She was thus able to obtain effects of differing textures which in fact correspond perfectly to the medium employed.

356 Simultaneous Contrasts. Poster design for a lecture. 1913. Coloured crayon on paper. 24.6 × 21 cm; no. 613.

Simultaneous Contrasts. Poster design for a lecture. 1913. Watercolour. 28.7 × 23.7 cm; no. 622. Musée National d'Art Moderne, Paris. 357

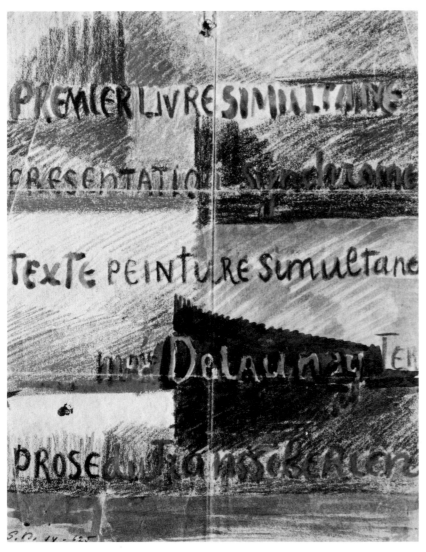

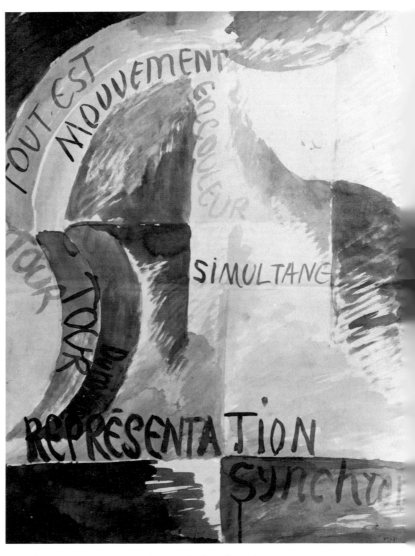

Sketch for a poster for the first 'simultaneous' book,
La Prose du Transsibérien by Blaise Cendrars.
1913. Watercolour and coloured crayon on paper.
25.3 × 19.8 cm; no. 625. Musée National d'Art Moderne, Paris.

Simultaneous Contrasts. Poster design for a lecture.
1913. Watercolour on paper. 64 × 49.2 cm; no. 471.

Simultaneous Contrasts. 1913. Coloured ink on paper. 14 × 20 cm; no. 470. Musée National d'Art Moderne, Paris.

Endpapers and binding for Blaise Cendrar's *Pâques à New York*.
1913. Endpapers, coloured paper cut-outs; binding, collage on suede.
25 × 15 cm; no. 652. Musée National d'Art Moderne, Paris.

361

Sketches of poster for Zenith watches.
1913. Oil on canvas. 30.5 × 38 cm; no. 890.
1914. Coloured inks and crayon. 14.4 × 21.7 cm; no. 490.
1913-1914. Coloured crayon. 19.9 × 25.5 cm; no. 489.

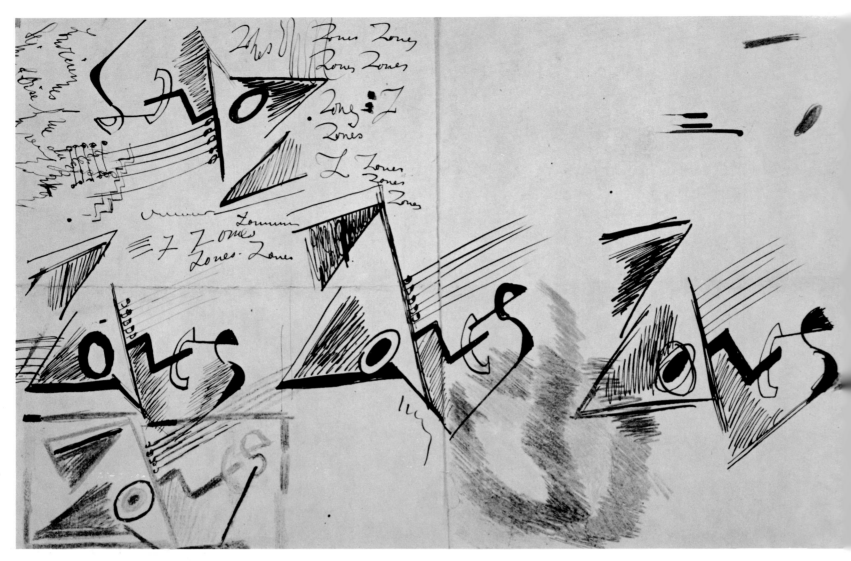

Studies for Apollinaire's poem *Zone*. 1912-1913. Indian ink and coloured crayon. 32 × 50 cm; no. 1456.

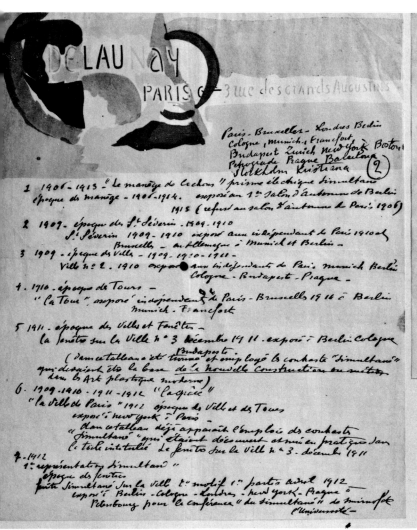

Letter-head for Robert and Sonia Delaunay. 1913. *Pochoir.*

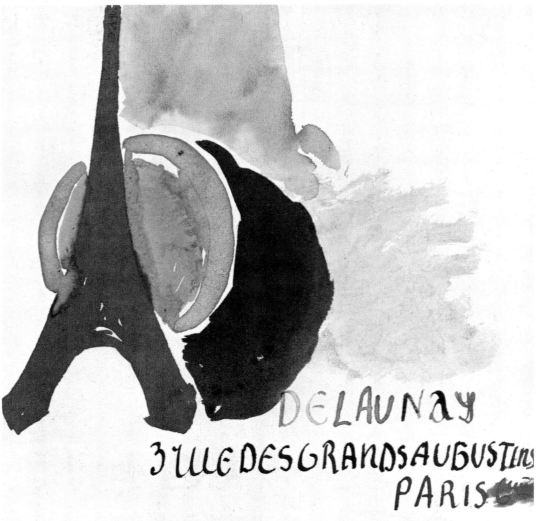

Studies for letter-heads
for Robert and Sonia Delaunay.
1913. Watercolour. Private collection, Pari
Sonia takes up Robert Delaunay's
theme of the Eiffel Tower.

Poster designs.

Chocolate. 1914.
Wax on paper. 36.3 × 44 cm; no. 611.
Musée National d'Art Moderne, Paris.

Zenith. 1914.
Distemper on paper. 34.9 × 30.5 cm; no. 495.
The 'Zenith' series seems to have influenced
Lissitzky's Z-shaped compositions.

Poster designs. Chocolate, 1922.
Below right: watercolour. 28 cm diameter; no. 1012.

Poster design. Dubonnet. 1914.
Cut out and pasted paper. 32.5 × 46.5 cm.
Musée National d'Art Moderne, Paris.

Poster design. Pencil. 1918. Watercolour. 16 × 12 cm.

375

Self-portrait for cover of the Stockholm catalogue. Portugal, 1916. Wax on paper. 64 × 32 cm; no. 119. Private collection, New York.

Final version of the
Stockholm catalogue cover, 1916.
Wax on paper. 33.7 × 45.7 cm.
Musée National d'Art Moderne,
Paris.

Cover designs for *Vogue* magazine. Vigo, 1916. Watercolour on paper. 35 × 23.5 cm.

Poster design. Pirelli. Paris, 1913. Pastel on paper. 20 × 26 cm.

Project for illuminated sign. Zig-Zag. 1935

E.A.

SD

Sonia Delaunay

382

Etching. Artist's proof.

over design for André Salmon's
ropos d'atelier. 1922. Gouache.

Poster design. Exhibition of Russian-born artists.
1945. Coloured crayon. 30.8 × 23.8 cm.

Cover design for *Album no. 1*. 1916. Wax on paper.

ALLA
COLOMB
VENEZIA

Prizewinning menu design for the restaurant Alla Colombo, Venice. 1960. 35 × 32 cm.

385

Zenith. Paris, 1914. *Papiers collés*, text by Cendrars.
66 × 81 cm. Musée National d'Art Moderne, Paris.

Sonia Delaunay 1936

on; Oriflamme.　Lithographs.

Four plates from Jacques Damase's book *Rythme-couleur*. *Pochoir*.

lack and White no. 2.
970.　Lithograph after a fabric design of 1936.

389

Proof sheet of the 'simultaneous' playing-cards, designed by Sonia Delaunay in 1960-1964. Spielkartenmuseum, Bielefeld.

First design for the king of clubs. 1938. Gouache. 48.5 × 17 cm; no 63. Spielkartenmuseum, Bielefeld.

391

392

Designs for court cards. 1964. Spielkartenmuseum, Bielefeld.

393

Two cards from
the 1964 pack.

396　Plate from *L'Alphabet*, poems by Jacques Damase. Milan, 1969.

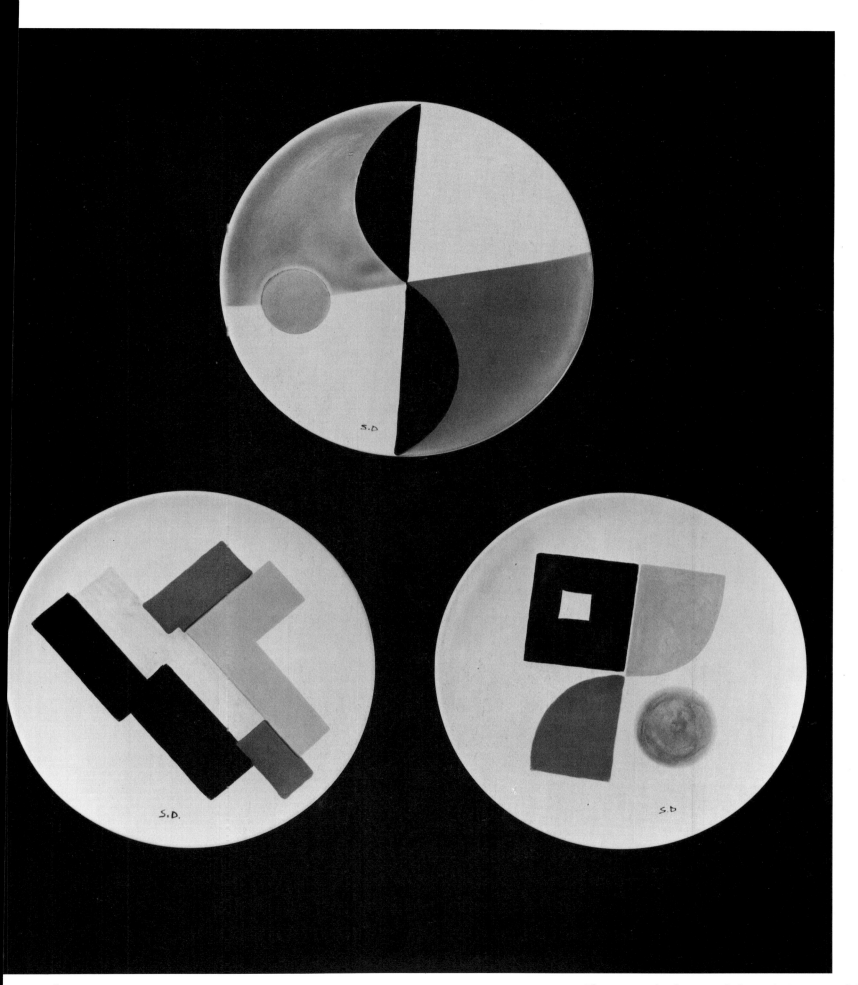

Three ceramic plates made in Turin in 1969.   397

398

ielefeld. 1958. Carpet. Mairie, Montpellier.

Black squares. 1967-1968. Carpet

925'. 1967-1968. Carpet.

Red squares. 1967-1968. Carpet.

lue and red carpet. 1967-1968. Musée du Havre.

Conclusion: Invention and Creation

Sonia Delaunay's work was always closely connected with that of her husband. From the very beginning, both conceived painting as a continuous process of research: Robert Delaunay when he began studying Chevreul's theories while still under the influence of Neo-Impressionism and of Seurat, and Sonia when she became inspired by the quality of light in the Iberian peninsula. Their entire work can be considered a prolongation of these early investigations. With a modesty that can only be admired, Sonia Delaunay has always stood aside in order to bring to the fore her late husband's works. Yet the most authoritative critics of Robert Delaunay's work have never failed to note the role played by his wife in his own evolution. Her work in the so-called minor fields of art, her experiments with new media and unexpected combinations of colour and materials, all resulted in the most original artefacts of pure colour.

As Francastel stressed (*XX*e *Siècle,* Christmas 1960), her creative role must not be underestimated: 'From the beginning of her career, she took part in all Delaunay's researches — and the expression "taking part" is still not strong enough. She herself carried out many of the experiments which led Delaunay first to define his theory of "simultaneity" and then to formulate the laws of a dynamic art of colour. Even if Sonia Delaunay's own work had not been so closely connected to that of her husband, it would undoubtedly and quite independently take its place among those works of art which have influenced their times. . . .

'Sonia Delaunay's . . . influence upon the art of her times is profound, and in particular, she played a most important part in establishing colour as one of the dominant features of modern art. Thanks to her, this avant-garde art so long misunderstood has entered our daily lives through materials, fashion, decors and book styles. We are confronted here with the transformation of public taste. A transformation which took place with remarkable ease and rapidity at an epoch when the hostility to modern art, led by a series of narrow-minded critics, was at its peak. One day, when a careful study of the evolution of twentieth-century taste is undertaken, it will become possible to retrace the broad lines of the common evolution of art, fashion, and theatre which, together, have created the styles of today. It will then become obvious that the so-called opposition of society (and in particular of French society) to changes in taste, is nothing but a false assertion on the part of critics and of so-called historians of present-day art. It will also become evident that the Delaunays, and more especially Sonia Delaunay, have influenced the art of a society which still remains largely ignorant of their name.

'Robert Delaunay was profoundly conscious both of his wife's support in the realization and transmission of their common ideas, and of the intrinsic quality of her own work as a painter.

'It is only today that the full impact and novelty of Sonia Delaunay's research, so patiently pursued all those years, is being felt by the younger generation. For many years, artists would not admit her influence, or at most were only superficially aware of it while at the same time being held under the spell of her paintings. It is only today that the true value of this work, which takes the form of an investigation into the countless possibilities of colour, can be measured. . . .

'In the last ten years, the role played by the Delaunays has slowly revealed itself even to the most blind. . . . As it appears, the Delaunays' art has still not been fully understood, not only because they impose a very personal style on their works, but more particularly because they offer an answer to some of the fundamental problems of present-day art, and because they suggest something which up until now has only been vaguely perceived; that is to say, a theory of modern painting which compels a complete rethinking of the values which were accepted in the first half of this century.'

Sonia Delaunay has always been an avant-garde artist, whether in 'pure art', in theatre, in fashion (the originality of her ideas were forty years ahead of those of Saint-Laurent and Courrèges), in advertising (already in 1914 Cassandre made use of her famous discs), in decoration and in a new conception of modern life. In 1930 she forecast the coming of ready-made haute couture clothes *(prêt-à-porter)*, and realized that one of the first requirements of a flat would one day be the built-in cupboard with prefabricated elements that can be added to it. She foresaw many other innovations decades before they even came into use. 'L'Exposition 1925', at the Musée des Arts Décoratifs in 1965, was the first historical evaluation of those times. Every epoch bequeathes two aspects of itself to posterity, and neither was absent from this exhibition: the one a caricature, branded with ridicule; the other forward-looking and destined to become classic. In the second category were the avant-garde achievements of artists like Sonia Delaunay and of movements such as the Bauhaus.

It is to Sonia Delaunay that we owe the first 'constructional' fabric designs. It was she who first used abstract designs on material. She invented, so to speak, new colour relationships, which created a new fashion. Above all she avoided those life-less symbols so dear to decorative artists of the times, those motifs borrowed from flowers, fruits or landscapes; instead, she concentrated on simple modern designs, figures of discs, segments, etc., which she unified through chromatic rhythms. Thanks to her, and also to the women who wore her dresses and her materials, modern art became part of everyday life.

The two spectacular exhibitions held in New York in 1965 — the one, 'The Responsive Eye' at the Museum of Modern Art, the other, 'Seven Decades: 1895-1965' organized by the Association for Public Education — falsified origins or, like so many others, simply ignored them. Though Matisse was vaguely referred to, in the preface of the catalogue, as a leader, as far as colour and theories were concerned, the Delaunays were never once mentioned, even in the context of Chevreul's writings on 'simultaneous' colour.

Yet, it is quite obvious where the works of painters such as Piero Dorazio, Frank Stella, Morris Louis, Kenneth Noland, Jasper Johns, Ad Reinhardt, Franz Marc, Larry Poons, Ellsworth Kelly, and many others, took their inspiration.

In terms of pure colour, the dissonances discovered by these two great artists are reappearing more and more frequently. But there is a fundamental difference between the original works and those they have inspired: the new works are devoid of all sensitivity. Most of the young artists have not yet understood the poetry of modernity. There have been examples of perfection, such as the works of Vasarely; but these have lacked human warmth. It is not that the younger generation is dishonest; rather, it is ignorant, and culls ideas here and there, not bothering or else forgetting to find out their sources and what has conferred upon them their beauty and their power.

Have Bridget Riley and Peter Sedgley of London realized that it was not they who invented Op Art and black-and-white art? They may know Vasarely, but are they aware that Sonia Delaunay had already carried out similar experiments round about 1930? Does Vieira da Silva know of Robert Delaunay's *City No. 2* which has for many years been exhibited at the Musée National d'Art Moderne, in Paris? One already finds in this painting all the fragmentation of forms and colours, which Vieira da Silva uses in her views of railway stations. This of course does not reduce the artist's talent, any more than the Cubists can be said to have plagiarized Cézanne's ideas. But if Cézanne's influence is recognized, why should that of the Delaunays be so carefully hidden?

This is a period of assimilation and integration. The original spark is no longer perceptible, and runs counter to a way of thinking which finds it difficult to consider as avant-garde something that has existed for decades. It is only just to pay our debt at last to the Delaunays to whom we owe these undulating forms, these harlequins, these rhythms with no end and no beginning.

Sonia Delaunay admits to having had an inclination for mathematics in her youth: this shows in her paintings. Her calculations, additions, multiplications and divisions are always correct; there is never an error, for if there had been, the whole painting would have collapsed as easily as a sand castle. On the contrary, her ideas expand, laying the foundations of the next picture.

I was once given the opportunity to see some of these 'syncopated rhythms' emerge, and I was able to follow their evolution from the small gouache she sometimes used as a starting point, or from the small rudimentary outline in charcoal. I had the luck to watch the first brush-stroke, the first colours being laid. Sometimes Sonia Delaunay does not immediately manage to solve her equation, and seeks the answer relentlessly, sometimes frenziedly, sometimes calmly. At times the painting becomes a battlefield of opposing forces — the enemy, a yellow or a green that is far too tenacious. Sometimes it turns into a game of chess: move one piece, one form, one colour, and everything has changed, everything must be worked out all over again. It is a fascinating procedure to watch.

Everywhere, at the moment, there are attempts at false revolutions. Art has become, in some people's minds, as unstable and frivolous a thing as a fashion which changes from one week to the next. But true painting, true values, sometimes submerged by all the nonsense, always surface again. Real painting, the only kind that matters, is made up of colours and rhythms, and of the poetry which lives in those rhythms.

The sometimes oblique statement to rhythm, the almost Dionysiac magic which brings the surface to life, are intersected by cross-rhythms and cross-currents; and the resulting syncopations are the living expression of our age of chaos and precision. As the painting progresses, as it gains ground, it is transformed.

As I watched, the centre and right-hand part of the painting, which had taken on something of the form of a triptych, seemed to collide head-on with the wave movements coming from the left. The work was still a labyrinth.

At another moment it shifted like the successive shots of a film. Everyone knows how much the construction of certain paintings, and the artists' use of light, have been an inspiration to film directors.

Another time, the painting seemed borne up by two wings, like a bird. An Icarus ready to take flight. Then the bird, the work, banked to the right, leaning its weight on the right wing. In the end the separation between the central mass and the two other parts disappeared. What remained was the deliberate dissonances, the syncopated rhythms which, after an interval of freedom and autonomy, bowed once more to the will of their tamer, the artist.

Phases of hesitation, doubt, weariness, like those of a mother dealing with a fractious child, were followed by enthusiasm, the pleasure of seeing the work respond at last. Sonia Delaunay's rectangles, triangles, squares and curves enchant the beholder through a dynamism which belongs to her alone. From elements which in their nature are rigid and cold, she creates a painting which is as warm and sunny as life ought always to be.

She is always a magician, sometimes a *Pierrot lunaire;* what she does is all gesture, rhythm and colour, dazzling in its eternal youth. The heart is not only red; it is all colours — in Joseph Delteil's phrase, the colours of the heart. It is the sacred heart, the loving heart, the heart pierced with thorns, the beating heart. Every quarter of a second, every thousandth of a second, a rhythm gives us new life.

We are spellbound by undulating rhythms, like the sailors of old who thought they saw mermaids on the high seas. But when the artist turns once more to the straight line, and takes up the reins, she amazes us with perfect equilibrium. Rational in the irrational, she sets up trajectories of sensibility, married to pure colour. This is the vision of the eyes and of the mind: the art of the future, prefigured decades ahead of its time.

'With the Delaunays,' writes Francastel, 'the qualitative representation of a movement — direction-velocity-shimmer captured in motion — takes its place in the basic vocabulary of contemporary art.'

Chromatic structure; inner language; poetry itself: all is expressed in the seemingly simple dance of a checkerboard pattern — for those who have eyes to see, and a heart to feel, the nature of rhythms and colours.

Chronology

compiled by Michel Hoog

1885	14 November, birth of Sonia Terk in the Ukraine.
1890	Adopted by her maternal uncle she goes to St. Petersburg where she spends her childhood and youth.
1903	Studies drawing under Schmidt-Reuter in Karlsruhe.
1905	Arrives in Paris, registers at the Académie de la Palette ; among her fellow-students are Ozenfant, Dunoyer de Segonzac and Boussingault.
1907	Her work is influenced by Fauvism and by Van Gogh and Gauguin.
1909	Marries Wilhelm Uhde.
1910	Divorces Uhde and marries Robert Delaunay.
1911	Birth of their son Charles. First experiments with applique work.
1912	Apollinaire is their guest from November to mid-December. Creation of the first 'simultaneous' works, collages, pastels and book-covers.
1913	Meeting with Blaise Cendrars. Illustration of his poem *La Prose du Transsibérien et de la petite Jehanne de France*. First 'simultaneous' dresses and waistcoats. Sends twenty paintings and objects to the Berlin Herbstsalon.
1914	Exhibits the *Electric Prisms* (Musée National d'Art Moderne, Paris) at the Salon des Indépendants. Holidaying in Spain when war is declared. They decide to settle in Madrid, as Charles is very ill (Robert Delaunay was discharged as unfit from the army in 1908).
1915	Departure for Portugal. Stay near Oporto in the company of American and Portuguese artists.
1916	They move tò Valença do Minho where she paints her series of *Portuguese Still-lifes* and her *Market in the Minho*.
1917	As a result of the Russian revolution, she loses her private income. She undertakes the decoration of the hall of the Petit Casino in Madrid and the costumes for its first floor-show. The Delaunays meet Serge de Diaghilev.
1918	Diaghilev returns to Madrid and commissions from the Delaunays the stage sets and costumes for *Cléopâtre*. He moves in with them at Sitges, with Massine and Lopouchova. On their return to Madrid they meet Stravinsky, Manuel de Falla and Nijinsky.
1920	They return to Paris to settle there for good, and make friends with writers and poets of the Surrealist group.
1922	Her first 'simultaneous' scarves.
1923	A Lyon silk manufacturer commissions her first 'simultaneous' materials. She designs and makes the costumes for Tristan Tzara's play *Le Cœur à gaz*.
1924	She decides to launch her own creations in 'simultaneous' materials and begins to make woollen tapestry coats. Joseph Delteil's poem 'La Mode qui vient' declaimed at the Hôtel Claridge; costumes by Sonia Delaunay.
1925	Publication of an album of her works. In collaboration with Jacques Heim displays her work in a boutique at the Exhibition of Decorative Arts.
1929	Publication of the album *Tissus et tapis*.

1930-1935	Concentrates almost entirely on her painting. Plays an active role in several groups which defend abstract painting.
1935-1937	Works on vast murals for the 1937 International Exhibition, and is awarded a gold medal.
1939	Robert and Sonia Delaunay organize meetings every Thursday, at which Robert lectures on modern art to young artists and architects. With the help of Rambosson, Fredo Sidès and Nelly Van Doesburg, they organize the first Salon des Réalités Nouvelles at the Charpentier gallery.
1941	Gravely ill, Robert Delaunay is operated on at Clermont-Ferrand. They then go down to Montpellier where Robert dies on 25 October. Sonia joins Jean Arp, Sophie Taeuber-Arp and Alberto Magnelli at Grasse. There she continues to paint. She remains in Grasse until 1944.
1944	Three-month stay in Toulouse with friends.
1946	Fredo Sidès asks her to help him organize the first post-war Salon des Réalités Nouvelles.
1949	André Farcy, curator of the Grenoble museum, asks her permission to organize an exhibition in homage to Robert Delaunay; it is then transformed into the exhibition 'Les Premiers maîtres de l'art abstrait' at the Maeght gallery in Paris.
1953	Exhibition of her works at the Bing gallery. From now on she participates in exhibitions the world over.
1958	Important exhibition of her works at Bielefeld. Execution of four *pochoirs* for Tzara's poem 'Le fruit permis'.
1959	Important exhibition of the works of both Delaunays at the Musée des Beaux-arts, Lyon.
1960	Important exhibition of the works of both Delaunays at Turin.
1961	Publication of Tristan Tzara's *Juste présent* with eight coloured engravings by Sonia Delaunay. Album of six coloured lithographs published by Pagani in Milan.
1962	Album of six *pochoirs* by Sonia Delaunay, published by Denise René, Paris. First exhibition of Sonia Delaunay's graphic works mounted by Pierre Berès, Paris.
1964	The Delaunay Donation to the Musée National d'Art Moderne comprising forty-nine works by Robert Delaunay and fifty-eight by Sonia Delaunay, is exhibited at the Louvre, Paris.
1965	First important exhibition in North America (Montreal, Toronto, Winnipeg, Regina, Quebec and Ottawa). Designs of materials and clothes are exhibited at the Pavillon de Marsan at the retrospective exhibition of the year 1925.
1966	Stained glass windows for the church of Saux at Montpezat (Lot-et-Garonne). Two tapestries are woven at the Gobelin state tapestry factory.
1967	After a gap of thirty years she designs some carpets. Important retrospective exhibition at the Musée National d'Art Moderne, Paris. Decoration of a Matra 530 car.
1968	Numerous lithographs. Decor and costumes for Stravinsky's *Danses concertantes* (Amiens).
1969	Publication of *L'Alphabet*. Text by Jacques Damase.
1970	Official visit of President Pompidou to the United States, where he presents President Nixon with a painting by Sonia Delaunay.
1971	First comprehensive exhibition of fabrics, at the Mulhouse Musée de l'Impression sur Etoffes.

Bibliographical Note

The majority of texts on Sonia Delaunay published before 1967 have been listed in the catalogue of the Robert and Sonia Delaunay donation (Paris, Musées Nationaux, *Inventaire des collections publiques françaises*, no. 15, 1967), compiled by Michel Hoog. The catalogue also contains a very full list of exhibitions up to that date.

Index

Page references in *italic* refer to illustrations.

412